FREE THE DUMB

THE TRUTH ABOUT FREEDOM IN AMERICA

FREE THE DUMB

THE TRUTH ABOUT FREEDOM IN AMERICA

William Wallace

Public Investigator

BALBOA.
PRESS

A DIVISION OF HAY HOUSE

Balboa Press books may be ordered through booksellers or by contacting:

Balboa Press
A Division of Hay House
1663 Liberty Drive
Bloomington, IN 47403
www.balboapress.com
1-(877) 407-4847

Because of the dynamic nature of the Internet, any Web addresses or links contained in this book may have changed since publication and may no longer be valid. The views expressed in this work are solely those of the author and do not necessarily reflect the views of the publisher, and the publisher hereby disclaims any responsibility for them.

The author of this book does not dispense medical advice or prescribe the use of any technique as a form of treatment for physical, emotional, or medical problems without the advice of a physician, either directly or indirectly. The intent of the author is only to offer information of a general nature to help you in your quest for emotional and spiritual well-being. In the event you use any of the information in this book for yourself, which is your constitutional right, the author and the publisher assume no responsibility for your actions.

Any people depicted in stock imagery provided by Thinkstock are models, and such images are being used for illustrative purposes only.

Certain stock imagery © Thinkstock.

ISBN: 978-1-4525-3182-3 (sc)
ISBN: 978-1-4525-3183-0 (e)

Library of Congress Control Number: 2010919154

Printed in the United States of America

Balboa Press rev. date: 1/18/2011

ASK AND YOU SHALL RECEIVE

For best results read this out loud with enthusiasm.

"I request a most benevolent outcome for having moral courage, to stand up for what is right and for reading, understanding, and using the material in this book. May the benefits be even more than I expect or anticipate. Thank you, thank you, thank you."

"I ask that any and all beings assist every American to embrace this book and that it helps every American fulfill their destiny and may it be the most benevolent outcome for them. Thank you, thank you, thank you."

DEDICATION

This book is dedicated to God, the Angels, Spirit Guides, George Washington, Benjamin Franklin, all of the rest of the Founding Fathers, my parents, everyone who so generously helped and anyone who has fought for truth and freedom.

DISCLAIMER

With the 1st Amendment of the Constitution, I don't understand why you need a disclaimer. The reason I am putting together these reports in this book is because it took me forty-five years to finally figure out that just about everything I had learned was all wrong. Will Rogers said, "It's not what you don't know that hurts you, it's what you know that ain't so." Orville Wright said, "If we were to accept as truth everything we were told to be true, there would be little hope for the human race." Helen Keller signed, "Don't believe anything you see, anything you hear, and only half of what you feel." This book is simply offering the readers information on various subjects for educational purposes and does not constitute any professional, medical, legal, or tax advice. I do not have a license for anything. All materials in this book are written in good faith with no intent to mislead or harm anyone. This publication does not condone the violation of any legitimate laws of these united States of America. To be truly free you must seek the truth. Truth always has been and always will be the same. It never changes. The hardest part of finding the truth is admitting to your ego that you don't know it.

CONTENTS

BULLETPROOF GEORGE WASHINGTON'S VISION

During the French and Indian War on July 9, 1755, seven miles from Fort DuQuesne, now Pittsburg, 1,300 English and American troops marching through a wooded ravine were ambushed. Within two hours, 714 of them were shot down. The French and Indians only lost 30 men. Out of 86 officers, George Washington was the only officer not shot down. In the history books for 150 years, on July 17, 1755 at Fort Cumberland, Western Maryland, a letter was sent to his brother said "By all the powerful dispensations of Providence, I have been protected by all human probability or expectations; I had four bullets through my coat, and two horses shot from under me and was not hurt."

In 1770, an Indian Chief at the battle came to meet him and said "I have traveled a long and weary path that I might see the young warrior of the great battle. I have come to pay homage to the man who is the particular favorite of Heaven, and who can never die in battle. I ordered my men to shoot down the officers. After shooting at you seventeen times, I told my men to stop shooting at you."

In the American Revolutionary War, approximately less than 3% of the three-million people in the colonies actually took part in the fight for American Independence.

Once the Declaration of Independence had been signed and Washington's forces were pitted against the British, his army was so greatly outnumbered and so ill equipped that many thought him foolhardy to even attempt to fight the most powerful nation in the world. Seldom in all of history has such a task been undertaken under such unfavorable conditions. However, Patrick Henry in his famous "Give me liberty or give me death" speech hit directly upon his reasons for hoping for ultimate victory when he said, "God will raise up friends to fight our battles for us."

General Washington led his men with a passion, courage and fortitude that could come only from total dedication. When the Continental Congress did not, or could not, send the funds for his soldiers' supplies and salaries, Washington paid for them out of his own pocket. He gained and held the allegiance of his men because he was fair, firm, resolute and dedicated. Moreover, he was a devoutly Christian man who made no apology for prayer. He repeatedly called upon God for deliverance and victory in the struggle for freedom.

George Washington believed that God would lead him to victory, and anyone who has read his handwritten letters and documents cannot help but be impressed by his reliance on the Almighty and deep belief in Divine Guidance.

Thomas Jefferson best expressed the relationship between man's highest aspiration and the great Creator when he wrote, "God who gave us life, gave us liberty." Throughout history, as is well documented in Holy Scripture and readily attested to by millions of observant people, God has raised up individuals, usually temporal leaders, to fulfill the destiny of men and nations.

Anthony Sherman, who was at Valley Forge in the cold winter of 1777, describes a situation: "You doubtless heard the story of Washington's going to the thicket to pray. Well, it is not only true, but he often used to pray in secret for aid and comfort from God, the interposition of whose Divine Providence brought us safely through the darkest days of tribulation."

"One day, I remember it well, when the chilly winds whistled through the leafless trees, though the sky was cloudless and the sun shown brightly, he remained in his quarters nearly all the afternoon alone. When he came out, I noticed that his face was a shade paler than usual. There seemed to be something on his mind of more than ordinary importance. Returning just after dusk, he dispatched an orderly to the quarters of the officer I mentioned, who was presently in attendance. After a preliminary conversation of about a half hour, Washington, gazing upon his companion with that strange look of dignity which he alone commanded, related the event that occurred that day."

George Washington said, "This afternoon, as I was sitting at this table engaged in preparing a dispatch, something seemed to disturb me. Looking up, I beheld standing opposite me a singularly beautiful female. So astonished was I, for I had given strict orders not to be disturbed, that it was some moments before I found language to inquire the cause of her presence. A second, a third and even a fourth time did I repeat my question, but received no answer from my mysterious visitor except a slight raising of her eyes.

By this time I felt strange sensations spreading through me. I would have risen but the riveted gaze of the being before me rendered volition impossible. I assayed once more to address her, but my tongue had become useless, as though it had become paralyzed.

A new influence, mysterious, potent, irresistible, took possession of me. All I could do was to gaze steadily, vacantly at my unknown visitor. Gradually the surrounding atmosphere seemed as if it had become filled with sensations, and luminous. Everything about me seemed to rarify, the mysterious visitor herself becoming more airy and yet more distinct to my sight than before. I now began to feel as one dying, or rather to experience the sensations which I have sometimes imagined accompany dissolution. I did not think, I did not reason, I did not move; all were alike impossible. I was only conscious of gazing fixedly, vacantly at my companion.

Presently I heard a voice saying, "Son of the Republic, look and learn," while at the same time my visitor extended her arm eastwardly. I now beheld a heavy white vapor at some distance rising fold upon fold. This gradually dissipated, and I looked upon a strange scene. Before my lay spread out in one vast plain all the countries of the world – Europe, Asia, Africa and America. I saw rolling and tossing between Europe and America the billows of the Atlantic and between Asia and America lay the Pacific.

"Son of the Republic," said the same mysterious voice as before, "look and learn". At that moment I beheld a dark, shadowy being, like an angel, standing, or rather floating in mid-air, between Europe and America. Dipping water out of the ocean in the hollow of each hand, he sprinkled some upon America with his right hand, while with his left hand he cast some on Europe.

Immediately a cloud rose from these countries, and joined in mid-ocean. For a while it remained stationary, and then moved slowly westward, until it enveloped America in its murky folds. Sharp flashed of lightning gleamed through it at intervals, and I heard the smothered groans and cries of the American people.

A second time the angel dipped water from the ocean, and sprinkled it out as before. The dark cloud was then drawn back to the ocean, in whose heaving billows it sank from view. A third time I heard the mysterious voice saying, "Son of the Republic, look and learn." I cast my eyes upon America and beheld villages and towns and cities springing up one after another until the whole land from the Atlantic to the Pacific was dotted with them.

Again I heard the mysterious voice say, "Son of the Republic, the end of the century cometh, look and learn." At this the dark shadowy angel turned his face southward, and from Africa I saw an ill-omened spectre approach our land. It flitted slowly over every town and city of the latter. The inhabitants presently set themselves in battle array against each other. As I continued looking I saw a bright angel, on whose brow rested a crown of light, on which was traced the word "Union," bearing the American flag, which he placed between the divided nation, and said, "Remember ye are brethren," Instantly, the inhabitants, casting from them their weapons became friends once more, and united around the National Standard.

And again I heard the mysterious voice say, "Son of the Republic, look and learn." At this the dark, shadowy angel placed a trumpet to his mouth, and blew three distinct blasts; and taking water from the ocean, he sprinkled it upon Europe, Asia, and Africa. Then my eyes beheld a fearful scene: from each of these countries arose thick, black clouds that were soon joined into one. Throughout this mass there gleamed a dark red light by which I saw hordes of armed men, who, moving with the cloud, marked by land and sailed by sea to America. Our country was enveloped in this volume of cloud, and I saw these vast armies devastate the whole country and burn the villages, towns and cities that I beheld springing up. As my ears listened to the thundering of the cannon, clashing of swords, and the shouts and cries of millions in mortal combat, I heard again the mysterious voice saying, "Son of the Republic, look and learn." When the voice had ceased, the dark shadowy angel placed his trumpet once more to his mouth, and blew a long and fearful blast.

Instantly a light as of a thousand suns shone down from about me, and pierced and broke into fragments the dark cloud which enveloped America. At the same moment the angel upon whose head still shone the word "Union", and who bore our national flag in one hand and a sword in the other, descended from the heavens attended by legions of white spirits. These immediately joined the inhabitants of America, who I perceived were well nigh overcome, but who immediately taking courage again, close up their broken ranks and renewed the battle.

Again, amid the fearful noise of the conflict, I head the mysterious voice saying, "Song on the Republic, look and learn." As the voice ceased, the shadowy angel for the last time dipped water from the ocean and sprinkled it upon America. Instantly the dark cloud rolled back, together with the armies it had brought, leaving the inhabitants of the land victorious!

Then once more I beheld the villages, towns and cities springing up where I had seen them before, while the bright angel, planting the azure standard he had brought in the midst of them, cried with a loud voice; "While the stars remain, and the heavens send down dew upon the earth, so long shall the "Union" last." And taking from his brow the crown on which blazoned the word, "Union," he placed it upon the Standard while the people, kneeling down, said, "Amen."

The scene instantly began to fade and dissolve, and I at last saw nothing but the rising, curling vapor I at first beheld. This also disappearing, I found myself once more gazing upon the mysterious visitor, who, in the same voice I had heard before, said, "Son of the Republic, what you have seen in thus interpreted: Three great perils will come upon the Republic. The most fearful is the third, but in this greatest conflict the whole world united shall not prevail against her. Let every child of the Republic learn to live for his God, his land and the "Union". With these words the vision vanished, and I started from my seat and felt that I had seen a vision wherein had been shown to me the birth, progress, and destiny of the United States".

George Washington's vision has been published from time to time and is recorded in the Library of Congress.

Lenin foretold the series of events: "First we will take Russia, next we will capture the nations of Eastern Europe, then we will take the masses of Asia. Finally, we will surround the United States and that last bastion of freedom will fall into our hands like over-ripe fruit."

In Washington's vision, he saw America attacked and invaded by vast military forces from Europe, Asia and Africa. He saw that with those forces there "gleamed a dark, red light" – the color and symbol of Communism. He saw our cities aflame (as a result of nuclear attack, burned by the invading enemy forces, or perhaps set afire by mobs fomenting anarchy and revolution); the whole nation devastated, and millions dying in mortal combat.

Then, at the point of fiercest and final battle, the great angel, the guardian of this nation, descended from the heavens with legions of white spirits that joined forces with the Americans and destroyed the invading armies.

A letter from Thomas Jefferson:

Monticello, January 2, 1814

I knew General Washington intimately and thoroughly; and were I called on to delineate his character; it would be in terms like these:

His mind was great and powerful, his penetration strong, and as far as he saw, no judgment was ever sounder. It was slow in operation, being little aided by invention or imagination, but sure in conclusion. Hence the common remark of his officers, of the advantage he derived from councils of war, where hearing all suggestions he selected whatever was best; and certainly no general ever planned his battles more judiciously.

He was incapable of fear, meeting personal dangers with the calmest unconcern. Perhaps the strongest feature in his character was prudence, never acting until every circumstance, every consideration, was maturely weighed; refraining if he saw a doubt, but when once decided, going through with his purpose, whatever obstacles opposed.

His integrity was most pure, his justice the most inflexible I have ever known, no motives of interest or consanguinity, of friendship or hatred, being able to bias his decision. He was, indeed, in every sense of the words, a wise, a good, and a great man.

His temper was naturally high toned; but reflection and resolution has obtained a firm and habitual ascendancy over it. If ever, however, it broke its bonds, he was most tremendous in wrath.

In his expenses he was honorable, but exact; liberal in contributions to whatever promised utility, but frowning and unyielding on all visionary projects and all unworthy projects and all unworthy calls on his charity. His heart was not warm in its affections; but he exactly calculated every man's value, and gave him a solid esteem proportioned to it.

His person, as you know, was fine, his stature exactly what one would wish, his deportment easy, erect and noble, the best horseman of his age, and the most graceful figure that could be seen on horseback.

He wrote readily, rather diffusely, in an easy and correct style. This he had acquired by conversation with the world, for his education was merely reading, writing, and common arithmetic, to which he added surveying at a later day. His time was employed in action chiefly.

On the whole, his character was, in its mass, perfect, in nothing bad, in few points indifferent; and it mat truly be said, that never did nature and fortune combine more perfectly to make a man great, and to place him in the same constellation with whatever worthies have merited from man by an everlasting remembrance.

For his was the singular destiny and merit of leading the armies of this country successfully through and arduous war, for the establishment of its independence; of conducting its councils through the birth of a government, new in its forms and principles, until it had settled down into a quiet and orderly train; and of scrupulously obeying the laws through the whole of his career, civil and military, of which the history of the world furnishes no other example...

Thomas Jefferson

Why do you think George Washington being bulletproof was taken out of the history books?

TREATS FROM PARIS

On July 4, 1776, the Founding Fathers signed the Declaration of Independence. But it wasn't until September 3, 1783 with the signing of the "Treaty of Paris" AKA "Peace of Paris" two years after the Revolutionary War that Americans got the birthright of a King. One reason it took so long is that the people wanted George Washington to be King. He said he did not defeat one King George for another King George. So in November of 1782, Prince Charles Edward Stewart AKA Charles III of Scotland was offered the Kingship. He declined because if he died without an heir, the House of Hanover would take over and the Revolutionary War would be for nothing. So on September 3, 1783, the greatest day on this continent, the Treaty of Paris was signed by Benjamin Franklin, John Adams and John Jay. In that, the Treaty of Paris and its two addendums signed by the King of England, the King of France, and the King of Spain, ceded their sovereignty to the people of America. This created a nation where all men had all the rights of a King, and that's a lot of rights.

"People of a State are entitled to all rights which formally belonged to the King by his prerogative."

Lansing vs. Smith (1892) 4 Wend. 9, 20.

Prerogative means "an exclusive right, a distinctive superior advantage."

"'The people, or the sovereign, are not bound by general words in statutes, restrictive of prerogative right, title or interest, unless expressly named. Acts of limitation do not bind the King nor the people. The people have ceded all the rights of the King, the former sovereign… It is a maxim of the common law, that when an active parliament is made for the public good, the advancement of the religion and justice, and to prevent injury and wrong, the King shall be bound by such an act, though not named, but when a statute is general, in any prerogative right, title or interest would be divested or taken from the King (or the people) in such case he shall not be bound."

The People vs. Herkimer 15 Am Dec 379, 4 Cowen (NY 345, 348, 1825).

"In the United States the people are sovereign and the government cannot sever its relationship to the people by taking away their citizenship."

Afroyim vs. Rusk 387 U.S. 253; 87 S.Ct. 1660 (May 29, 1967)

"There is no such thing as power of inherent sovereignty in the government of the United States… In this country sovereignty resides in the People, and Congress can exercise no such power in which [the sovereign People] have not, by their Constitution entrusted to it… All else is withheld."

Julliard vs.Greenman 10 U.S. 421 (March 3, 1884)

Definition… Sovereign (Webster) "Having supreme rank, power and authority… Supreme and independent power, indisputable… being about all others."

"You have rights antecedent to all earthly governments; rights that cannot be repealed or restrained by human law; Rights derived from the Great Legislature of the universe." John Adams, 2nd President of the United States.

YOU GOTTA KEEP THEM SEPARATED

George Washington, in a speech (May 12, 1779), said to the Delaware chiefs about bringing their youth to our schools, "You do well to wish to learn arts and way of life, and above all the religion of Jesus Christ. These will make you a greater and happier people than you are. Congress will do everything they can to assist you in this wise intention."

George Washington's Report to Congress (September 26, 1780) stated, "Treason of the blackest dye was yesterday discovered! General Arnold who commanded at West Point was about to deliver up that important post into the hands of the enemy. Such an event must have given the American cause a deadly wound if not a fatal stab. Happily, the treason has been timely discovered to prevent a fatal misfortune. The providential train of circumstances which led to it, affords the most convincing proof that liberties of America are the object of divine protection."

Robert Akin of Philadelphia on January 21, 1781 officially requested permission to print Bibles for use in school. It became the first Bible printed in America.

George Washington's Circular Letter (June 8, 1783) stated, "Without a humble imitation of the characteristics of the Divine Arthur of our blessed religion, we can never hope to be a happy nation."

Benjamin Franklin wrote to Thomas Paine in 1786, "You, yourself, may find it easy to live a virtuous life without the assistance afforded by religion. But think how great a proportion of mankind consists of weak and ignorant men and women, and the inexperienced and inconsiderate youth of both sexes, who have need of the motives of religion to restrain them from vice."

On June 7 – September 25, 1789, while working on the first Amendment the Northwest Ordinance was passed. The House passed it on July 7, 1789. The Senate passed it on August 4, 1789 and it was signed by George Washington and became a law on August 7, 1789. Article III states for a territory to become a state, schools had to teach knowledge, morality, and religion. It had to be in each states Constitution or the territory could not become a state.

Delaware Constitution: "Everyone appointed to public office shall say: I do profess faith in God the Father, and in the Lord Jesus Christ his only Son, and in the Holy Ghost, one God blessed for evermore; and I do acknowledge the Holy Scriptures of the Old and New Testament to be given by divine inspiration."

Pennsylvania and Vermont Constitutions: "Each member [of the legislature], before he takes his seat, shall make and subscribe the following declaration: I do believe in one God, the Creator and Governor of the universe, the rewarder of the good, and punisher of the wicked and I do acknowledge the Scriptures of the Old and New Testaments to be given by divine inspiration."

North Carolina Constitution: "No person who should deny the being of a God, or the truth of the [Christian] religion or the divine authority of either the Old or New Testaments, or who should hold religious principles incompatible with the freedom and safety of the State, should be capable of holding any office or place of trust in the civil government of this State."

Massachusetts Constitution: "All persons elected must make and subscribe the following declaration: I do declare that I believe the Christian religion and have firm persuasion of its truth."

An acknowledgment of Christian belief was a requirement of holding public office during the years of the Founding Fathers. Consistent with the 1st Amendment saying you didn't need to be as it was in Britain of one denomination to hold office, any denomination will do.

The Founding Fathers structured education after the way Martin Luther had recommended, saying "I am very much afraid that schools will prove to be the great gates of hell unless they diligently labor in explaining the Holy Scriptures, engraving them in the hearts of youth. I advise no one to place his child where the Scriptures do not reign paramount. Every situation in which men are not increasingly occupied with the Word of God must become corrupt."

William Penn said, "Governments, like clocks, go from the motion men give them wherefore governments rather depends upon men, than men depend on government's. Let men be good, and the government's cannot be bad. But, if men be bad, the government is never good. I know some say; let us have good laws, and no matter for the men that execute them but let them consider that good laws do well, good men do better: for good laws may lack good men but good men will never lack good laws, nor allow bad ones."

At the Constitutional Convention on June 28, 1787, Benjamin Franklin said, "We needed God to be our friend and our ally. We need to keep God's concurring aid. If a sparrow cannot fall to the ground without his notice, is it probable that an empire can rise without his aid? We've been assured in the sacred writing that, 'Except the Lord build the house, the labor in vain that build it.' " So he called for daily prayer to keep God in what was done for the nation.

The Founding Fathers pointed out that only religion could stop crime before it started because all crime comes out of the heart and if you could control the heart you could control the crime.

John Adams said, "We have no government armed with power capable of contending with human passions unbridled by morality and religion," and he said, "Our constitution was made only for moral and religious people. It is wholly inadequate to the government of any other." He also said, "Statesmen may plan and speculate for liberty, but it is religion and morality alone which can establish the principles upon each freedom can securely stand."

Elias Boudinot, President of the Constitutional Congress, said "Let us enter on this important business under the idea that we are Christians on whom the eyes of the world are now turned... Let us in the first place... humbly and penitently implore the aid of the Almighty God whom we profess to serve – let us earnestly call and beseech him for Christ's sake to preside in our councils." He also said, "If the moral character of a people once degenerate their political character must follow. These considerations should lead to an attentive solicitude to be religiously careful in our choice of all public officers... and judge of the tree by its fruits."

Patrick Henry, Founding Father, said, "It cannot be emphasized too strongly or too often that this great nation was founded, not by religionists, but Christians, not by religions, but on the gospel of Jesus Christ."

John Witherspoon, Founding Father, President of Princeton, taught his students what it meant to be a patriot and how to distinguish an American patriot. He said, "That he is the best friend to American liberty who is most sincere and active and promoting true and undefiled religion, and who sets himself with the greatest firmness to bare down profanity an immorality of every kind. Whoever is an avowed enemy to God, a scruple not to call him an enemy to his country."

Benjamin Rush, Founding Father, wrote in a letter published in a book called *A defense of the use of the Bible in schools*: Dear Sir, It is now several months since I promised to give you my reasons for preferring the Bible, as a schoolbook, to all other compositions. Before I state my arguments, I shall assume the five following propositions:

1. That Christianity is the only true and perfect religion; and that, in proportion as mankind adopt its principles, and obey its precepts, they will be wise and happy.

2. That a better knowledge of this religion is to be acquired by reading the Bible, in any other way.
3. That the Bible contains more knowledge necessary to man in his present state, than any other book in the world.
4. That knowledge is the most durable, and religious instruction most useful, when imparted in early life.
5. That the Bible, when not read in schools, is seldom in any subsequent period of life.

In the latter part he goes into what would happen if we got away from the Bible in schools writing: In contemplating the political institutions of the United States, I lament that we waste so much time and money in punishing crimes and take so little pains to prevent them. We profess to be Republicans, and yet we neglect the only means of establishing and perpetuating our republican forms of government; that is, the universal education of our youth in the principles of Christianity by the means of the Bible; for this Divine Book; above all others, favors that equality among mankind, that respect for just laws, and all those sober and frugal virtues constitute the sound of republicanism.

Fisher Ames, Founding Father, who entered Harvard University at age twelve and gave us the wording for the 1st Amendment wrote on the role of the Bible in school books: It has been the custom, of late years, to put a number of little books into the hands of children, containing fables and moral lessons. This is very well, because it is right first to raise curiosity, and then to guide it. Many books for children are, however, injudiciously compiled: (In closing wrote) Why then, if these books for children must be retained, as they will be, should not the Bible regain the place it once held as a school book? Its morals are pure; its examples captivating are noble. The reverence for the sacred book, that is thus early impressed, last long, and, probably, if not impressed in infancy, never takes firm hold of the mind.

Charles Finney said, "The church must take right ground in regard to politics. Politics are a part of a religion in such a country as this, and Christians must do their duty to the country as a part of their duty to God. God will bless or curse this nation, according to the course [Christians] taken politics."

First Supreme Court Justice John Jay said, "Providence has given our people the choice of their rulers, and it is the duty, as well as the privilege and interest, of our Christian nation, to select and prefer Christians for their rulers."

George Mason, Father of the Bill of Rights, said "As nations cannot be rewarded or punished in the next world, so they must be in this. By an inevitable chain of causes and effects, Providence punishes national sin by national calamities."

George Washington's Inaugural Address: "...the propitious smiles of Heaven can never be expected on a nation that disregards the eternal rules of order and right which Heaven itself has ordained; and since the preservation of the sacred fire of liberty and the destiny of the replication model of government are justly considered, perhaps, as deeply, as finally, state on the experiment and trusted to the hands of the American people."

Noah Webster, Founding Father, author of the dictionary, said "The religion which has introduced civil liberty is the religion of Christ and his apostle. This is genuine Christianity, and to this we owe are free constitutions of government." He also said, "The Christian religion is the most important and one of the first things in which all children under a free government ought to be instructed. The Christian religion must be the basis of any government intended to secure the rights and privileges of a free people."

Noah Webster instructed students: In selecting men for office, let principle be your guide. Regard not that the particular sect or denomination of the candidate – look to his character. It is alleged by men of lose principles, or defective views of the subject, that religion and morality are not necessary or important qualifications for public stations. The Scriptures teach a different doctrine. They direct that rulers should be men "who rule in the fear of God able men, such a fear of God, men of truth, hate covetousness." (From Exodus 18)

Noah Webster wrote in the book, *History of the United States,* The brief exposition of the constitution of the United States, will unfold to the young persons the principles of republican government; and it is the sincere desire of the writer that our citizens should early understand that the genuine source of correct republican principles is the Bible, particularly the New Testament, or the Christian religion. In the *Advice to the Young* section he wrote: The moral principles and precepts contained in the Scriptures ought to form the basis of all our civil constitutions and laws, all the miseries and evils which men suffer from vice, crime, ambition, injustice, oppression, slavery, and war proceed from the despising and neglecting the precepts contained in the Bible. After his death he was known as the man who taught millions to read but not one to sin.

Also in *History of the United States,* When you become entitled to exercise the right of voting for public officers, let it be impressed on your mind that God commands you to choose for rulers, "just men who will rule in the fear of God". The preservation of government depends on the faithful discharge of this duty; If the citizens neglect their duty and place unprincipled men in office, the government will soon be corrupted, laws will be made not for the public good so much for selfish or local purposes; Corruption of incompetent men will be appointed to execute the laws; the public revenues will be squandered on unworthy men; and the rights of the citizens will be violated or disregarded. If government fails to secure public prosperity and happiness, it must be because the citizens neglect the divine commands, and elect bad men to make and administer the laws.

Dr. Jedediah Morse, called the "Father of American Geography", wrote: To the kindly influence of Christianity we owe that degree of civil freedom and political and social happiness which mankind now enjoys. In proportion as the genuine affects of Christianity are diminished in any nation, in the same proportion will the people of that nation recede from the blessings of genuine freedom. I hold this to be a truth confirmed by experience, it follows that all efforts made to destroy the foundations of our holy religion ultimately tend to the subversion also of our political freedom and happiness. Whenever the pillars of Christianity shall be overthrown, our present republican forms of government, and all the blessings which flow from them must fall with them.

Samuel Adams, Founding Father of the American Revolution, leader of the Boston Tea Party and brewer, in a letter to John Adams on the subject of government on what needs to be done to keep America on a firm foundation, wrote, What then is to be done? Let divines and philosophers, statesmen and patriots, unite their endeavors to renovate the age, by impressing the minds of men with the importance of educating their little boys and girls; of inculcating in the minds of youth the fear and love of the Deity and universal philanthropy, and in subordination to these great principals, the love of their country; of instructing them in the art of self-government, without which they never can act a wise part in the government of societies, great or small; in short, of leading them in the study and practice of the exalted virtues of the Christian system, which will happily tend to subdue the turbulent passions of men. John Adams wrote back saying, Of this, you and I agree.

Thomas Jefferson said "And can the liberties of a nation be thought secure when we have removed their only firm basis – a conviction in the minds of the people that these liberties are the gift of God? That they are not to be violated but with his wrath? Indeed I tremble for my country when I reflect that God is just; that his justice cannot sleep forever."

For years, textbooks were all about Bible verses and questions on the Bible.

The New England Primer, 1690-1900

Early American Textbook – Office of Education, Research and
   Improvement, 1775-1900

Webster's Blue Book Speller, 1780-1930

U.S. Congressional Records June 7 – September 25, 1789 The Intent of the 1st Amendment was not to have one denomination running the nation.

Runkel vs. Winemiller – 1799 "By one form of government, the Christian religion is an established religion; and all sects and denominations of Christians are place on the same equal footing."

September 23, 1800 – A letter from Thomas Jefferson to Benjamin Rush:

President Jefferson committed himself to not allowed any one denomination to achieve the "establishment of a particular form of Christianity."

November 7, 1801 – A letter from the Danbury Baptist Association to President Jefferson:

They were concerned about "free exercise of religion" appearing in the 1st Amendment. To them, this implied the government had the power to regulate religious expression. They believed that freedom of religion was a God-granted, unalienable right, and that the government should be powerless to restrict religious activities unless those activities caused someone to "work ill to his neighbor."

Jefferson's letter to Danbury Baptist Association on January 1, 1802, stated that the 1st Amendment has erected a wall of separation between church and state, that government would not interfere with religion, and that religion was a God granted unalienable right not government granted.

The clear understanding of the 1st Amendment was that it prohibited establishing a single national denomination. "Separation of church and state" appears in no founding documents.

President Jefferson plans of education for Washington D.C. public schools had two books: the Bible and Isaac Watts Hymn book, stating "I have always said, and always will say, that the studious perusal of the sacred volume will make us better citizens."

Reynolds vs. United States – October 1878 Danbury's letter was used to prove it meant one denomination. Charges in Everson vs. Board of Education 1947 took the Danbury letter out of context. Just using 8 words of the Danbury letter, the court ruled "The 1st Amendment has erected 'a wall of separation between church and state'. That wall must be kept high and impregnable."

James Wilson, Founding Father, an original Supreme Court justice said, "Human law must rest its authority ultimately upon the authority of that law which is Divine. Far from being rivals or enemies, religion and law are twin sisters. Indeed, these two scientists run into each other. The Divine law forms an essential part of both."

Ohio Constitution (1802) – Religion, morality, and knowledge, being essentially necessary to good government and the happiness of mankind, schools and the means of instruction shall forever be encouraged by legislative provision.

People vs. Ruggles (1811) Whatever strikes at the root of Christianity tends manifestly to the dissolution of civil government. The court ruled that an attack on Christianity was an attack on the foundation of the country and the court sentence was 3 months in jail and a $500 fine.

Mississippi Constitution (1817) – Religion, morality, and knowledge, being necessary to good government, the preservation of liberty and the happiness of mankind, schools and the means of education shall forever be encouraged in this state.

Daniel Webster said, "If we abide by the principles taught in the Bible our country will go on prospering, but if we neglect its instruction and authority, no man can tell how soon a catastrophe may welcome us, and burry all our glory in profound obscurity."

From the works of Daniel Webster: In Philadelphia a school was started to teach morality without religion. Daniel Webster argued in front of the Supreme Court for three days, the courts response was: Why may not the Bible, and especially the New Testament, be read and taught as a divine revelation in the schools? Its general precepts expounded, and its glorious principles of morality inculcated? Where can the purest principles of morality be learned so clearly or so perfectly as form the New Testament?

Vidal vs. Girard – (1844) Why may not the Bible, and especially the New Testament be read and taught as a Divine revelation in the [schools] – it's general precepts expounded and its glorious principles of morality inculcated? Where can the purest principles of morality be learned so clearly or so perfectly as from the New Testament?

House Judiciary Committee Report, March 27, 1854: Had the people during the Revolution, had a suspicion of any attempt to make war against Christianity, that the Revolution would have been strangled in its cradle. At the time of the adoption of the Constitution and the amendments, the universal sentiment was that Christianity should be encouraged, but not anyone sect [denomination]. In this age, there is no substitute for Christianity. That was the religion of the founders of the republic, and they expected it to remain the religion of their descendants.

Abraham Lincoln said "The philosophy of the school room in one generation will be the philosophy of government in the next," and when he heard someone say they hope God was on their side, he said "Sir, I am not at all concerned about that, for I know the Lord is always on the side of the right. But it is my constant anxiety and prayer that I and this nation should be on the Lord's side."

Nebraska Constitution (1875) – Religion, morality, and knowledge, however, being essential to good government it shall be the duty of the legislature to pass suitable laws to encourage schools and the means of instruction.

Rector, Etc., Of Holy Trinity Church v. United States, 143 U.S. 457; 12 S.Ct. 511 (Feb. 29, 1892)

"In construing a doubtful statute the court will consider the evil which it was designed to remedy, and for this purpose will look into contemporaneous events, including the situation as it existed, and as it was pressed upon the attention of the legislative body, while the act was under consideration."

"It being historically true that the American people are a religious people, as shown by the religious objects expressed by the original grants and charters of the colonies, and the recognition of religion in the most solemn acts of their history, as well as in the constitutions of the states and the nation, the courts, in construing statutes, should not impute to ant legislature a purpose of action against religion."

"It is a familiar rule that a thing may be within the letter of the statute and yet not within its spirit nor within the intention of its makers. This has been often asserted, and the Reports are full of cases illustrating its application. This is not the substitution of the will of the judge for that of the legislator; for frequently words of general meaning are used in a statute, words broad enough to include an act in question, and yet a consideration of the whole legislation, or of the circumstances surrounding its enactment, of the absurd results which follow from giving such broad meaning to the words, making it unreasonable to believe that the legislator intended to include the particular act."

"All laws should receive a sensible construction. General terms should be so limited in their application as not to lead to injustice, oppression, or an absurd consequence. It will always, therefore, be presumed that the legislature intended exceptions to its language which would avoid results of this character. The reason of the law in such cases should prevail over its letter. The common sense of man approves the judgment mentioned by Puffendorf, that the Bolognian law which enacted 'that whoever drew blood in the streets should be punished with the utmost severity,' did not extend to the surgeon who opened the vein of a person that fell down in the street in a fit. The same common sense accepts the ruling, cited by Plowden, that the statute of 1 Edw. II., which enacts that a prisoner who breaks prison shall be guilty of felony, does not extend to a prisoner who breaks out when the prison is on fire, 'for he is not to be hanged because he would not stay to be burnt.' US vs. Kirby, 7 Wall. 482, 486.

In the case of US vs. Fisher, 2 Cranch, 358, 386, Chief Justice Marshall said: "…Where the intent is plain, nothing is left to construction. When the mind labors to discover the design of the legislature, it seizes everything from which aid can be derived; and in such case the title claims a degree of notice, and will have its due share of consideration." And in the case of US vs. Palmer, 3 Wheat. 610, 631, the same judge applied the doctrine in this way: "The words of the section are in terms of unlimited extent. The words 'any person or persons' are broad enough to comprehend every human being. But general words must not only be limited to cases within the jurisdiction of the state, but also to those objects to which the legislature intended to apply them. Did the legislature intend to apply these words to the subjects of a foreign power, who in a foreign ship may commit murder or robbery on the high seas? The title of an act cannot control its words, but may furnish some aid in showing what was in the mind of the legislature. The title of this act is, 'An act for the punishment of certain crimes against the United States.' It would seem that offenses against the United States, not offenses against the human race, were the crimes which the legislature intended by this law to punish."

"It will be seen that words as general as those used in the first section of this act were by that decision limited, and the intent of congress with respect to the act was gathered partially, at least, from its title. Now, the title of this act is, "An act to prohibit the importation and migration of foreigners and aliens under contract or agreement to perform labor in the United States, its territories, and the District of Columbia. Obviously the thought expressed in this reaches only to the work of the manual laborer, as distinguished from that of the professional man. No one reading such a title would suppose that Congress had in its mind any purpose of staying the coming into this country of ministers of the gospel, or, indeed, of any class whose toil is that of the brain. The common understanding of the terms "labor" and "laborers" does not include preaching and preachers, and it is to be assumed that words and phrases are used in their ordinary meaning. So whatever of light is thrown upon the statute by the language of the title indicates and exclusion from its penal provisions of all contracts for the employment of ministers, rectors, and pastors."

"It was never suggested that we had in this country a surplus of brain toilers, and, least of all, that the market for the services of Christian ministers was depressed by foreign competition."

"Especially would the committee have otherwise recommended amendments, substituting for the expression, 'labor and service,' whenever it occurs in the body of the bill, the words 'manual labor' or 'manual services,' as sufficiently broad to accomplish the purposes of the bill, and that such amendments would remove objections which a sharp and perhaps unfriendly criticism may urge to the proposed legislation. The committee, however, believing that the bill in its present form will be construed as including only those whose labor or service is manual in character, and being very desirous that the bill become a law before the adjournment, have reported the bill without change.""

"Even the Constitution of the United States, which is supposed to have little touch upon the private life of the individual, contains in the 1st Amendment a declaration common to the Constitutions of all the states, as follows: "Congress shall make no law respecting an establishment of religion, or prohibiting the free exercise thereof," etc.,--and also provides in Article 1, Section 7, (a provision common to many constitutions,) that the executive shall have 10 days (Sundays excepted) within which to determine whether he will approve or veto a bill."

"There is no dissonance in these declarations. There is a universal language pervading them all, have one meaning. They affirm and reaffirm that this is a religious nation. These are not individual saying, declarations of private persons. They are organic utterances. They speak the voice of the entire people."

The court provided 87 precedents and said it could provide more but explained that 87 was enough to conclude that we were a Christian nation.

From the Education Teachers Union Book, 1892:

In the beginning, University and grade school education was nurtured in the churches. As the classes grew the churches volunteered to relinquish grade school education to the State. Whether this

was wise or not it is not my purpose to discuss, further than to remark that, if the study of the Bible is to be excluded from all State schools, if the inculcation of the principles of Christianity is to have no place in the daily programme, if the worship of God is to form no part of the general exercises of these public elementary schools, then the good of the State would be better served by restoring all schools to church control. Of the first 126 colleges, 123 were founded on Christianity. In 1900, it was very rare to find a president of the University that was not a clergyman. Founding Fathers said, "If you were an enemy of God, you were an enemy of America."

Engel vs. Vitale (June 25, 1962) – The Unconstitutional Prayer which led to the removal of all prayer in American schools was "Almighty God, we acknowledge our dependence upon Thee, and we beg Thy blessing upon us, our parents, our teachers and Country."

So after 300 years, school prayer was ruled unconstitutional.

Under the Constitution, the court defined "church" as being a federally established denomination. The 1962 case redefined "church" to mean any religious activity performed in public unconstitutional. This definition is brand new. There were no precedents. It is not from the Founding Fathers. It was the first case in history not to quote any previous legal cases or historical incidents. This is the first time that 3% was ruled as a majority.

Since the "separation of church and state", America's number one in the world in violent crime, divorce, voluntary abortion, and drug use. In the western world number one in teen pregnancy and illiteracy.

Baer v. Kolmorgen (1958) A dissenting judge warned that continuing talk about the "separation of church and state" would make people think it was part of the Constitution.

"Separation of church and state" is not a teaching of the Founding Fathers, it is a historical teaching and until 1962, a teaching of law: it is not a Biblical teaching.

Torcas v. Watkins (1961 and 1985) ruled that Secular Humanism is a viable 1st Amendment religion. A religion that means God has no place in their philosophy.

Abington v. Schempp (1962) & Murray v. Curlett (1963) – These cases reaffirmed the band on school prayer and school Bible reading saying with no precedents, "If portions of the New Testament were read without explanation, they could be and had been psychologically harmful to the child."

Reed v. Van Hoven (1965) – Allow prayer over lunch in school as long as no one could tell it was a prayer.

Theriault v. Silber - Malank v. Yogi (1977) ruled atheism as a religion. Atheism means religiously practicing non-religion. Therefore not reading the Bible is a violation of "separation of church and state".

Stone v. Graham (1980) Supreme Court ruled that it was unconstitutional for a student to see a posted copy of the Ten Commandments saying "If the posted copies of the Ten Commandments are to have any effect at all, it will be to induce the school children to read, meditate upon, perhaps to venerate and obey the Commandments... this is not a permissible... objective."

The SAT was started in 1926 and remains the same test since 1941. Since 1963 the scores have continuously dropped. The Department of Education said on public schools, they are graduating a generation of students that know less than their parents taking the same SAT there is a drastic point difference. Prior to 1962, there were a thousand Christian private schools. Now there are tens of thousands. SAT scores are higher for private school students.

This nation was better off before the Department of Education was established in 1968. The first five years that the Federal Department of Education was in existence, College tuitions went up 2,000%. Why? Because the colleges across the country suddenly discovered they had your blank check book in their hands. Education should be facilitated on the state level without federal involvement. After your child graduates they are deep in debt. Our schools are not teaching the correct history by

teaching that the United States is a democracy. Children who are home schooled are graduating at the top of the class and their children do not have the social engineering that goes against their beliefs.

Benjamin Franklin said, "I believe in one God, Creator, of the Universe. That he governs it by his Providence. That he ought to be worshipped. That the most acceptable service that we render to him is doing well to his other children."

The way territories became States was to put in their Constitution that they would teach morality and religion and haven't done so since 1962. Should the States go back to being territories or should they be forced to teach morality and religion?

Since the churches relinquished their power to the States to teach the children on the same grounds, violating their Constitutional contract, should the churches take back the teaching of the children?

Other Court Cases:

- Robin vs. Hardaway, 1 Jefferson 109, (Va., 1772): "All acts of the legislature apparently contrary to natural rights and justice are, in our law and must be in the nature of things, considered void ... We are in conscience bound to disobey."
- U.S. v. Cheek – One cannot be punished for sincerely held religious convictions.

THE "MISSING LUCKY" 13TH AMENDMENT

"If any citizen of the United States shall accept, claim, receive, or retain any title of nobility or honour, or shall without the consent of Congress, accept and retain any present, pension, office, or emolument of any kind whatever, from any emperor, king, prince, or foreign power, such person shall cease to be a citizen of United States, and shall be incapable of holding any office of trust or profit under them, or either of them."

To have "titles of nobility" in government would be a direct conflict with the Declaration of Independence which was to break off from King George III's rule.

It was prohibited in Article VI of the Articles of Confederation which is still law under Article VI of the Constitution and in Article I, Section 9 of the Constitution of the United States of America.

The American Revolution provided an example and incentive for people of other countries to overthrow their monarchies as in the French Revolution 1789 to 1799 and the Polish uprising in 1794. The United States was destroying monarchies around the world.

The monarchies sought to destroy or subvert the American Republic in bribery and legal deception through the Jay Treaty, US Bank Charter and the Federalists pro-monarchy party. In an un-cataloged book titled "2 VA Law" it reveals a plan to overthrow the constitutional government by secret agreements engineered by lawyers of the time.

The only organization that certified lawyers in Colonial America was the International Bar Association chartered by the King of England. The lawyers received the rank in "Esquire" which was a "title of British nobility".

Lawyers are under the Judicial Branch of the government; therefore, if they were to be a part of the other branches, wouldn't that be a violation of the separation of powers.

The Articles of Confederation and the Constitution of the United States of America sought to prohibit these lawyers from operating in the American government but the Articles of Confederation and the Constitution of the United States of America failed to specify a penalty. So it was ignored, and agents of the monarchy infiltrated, influenced, and corrupted the government. The intent of the "missing lucky" 13th Amendment was to prohibit people having "titles of nobility" and loyalties to foreign governments from voting, holding public office and trying to subvert the government.

Senator Reed in January 1810 proposed the "missing lucky" 13th Amendment (History of Congress, Proceedings of the Senate, page 529-530). On April 17th, 1810, the Senate voted to pass it 26-1; the House voted 87-3 and was sent to the States for ratification. Ironically the "missing lucky" 13th Amendment needed thirteen states to make it a law. Twelve states ratified it, and their dates of ratification are:

Maryland, ----- Dec. 25, 1810 .... Vermont, ------ Oct. 24, 1811
Kentucky, ----- Jan. 31, 1811 .... Tennessee, ---- Nov. 21, 1811
Ohio, ---------- Jan. 31, 1811 .... Georgia, ------- Dec. 13, 1811
Delaware, ----- Feb. 2, 1811 .... North Carolina, -- Dec. 23, 1811
Pennsylvania, -- Feb. 6, 1811 .... Massachusetts, -- Feb. 27, 1812
New Jersey, --- Feb. 13, 1811 .... New Hampshire, -- Dec. 10, 1812

But before a thirteenth state could ratify it, the War of 1812 started. Some think the war was started to stop the ratification. The British burned the Capitol Building, the Library of Congress, and the Secretary of State Building holding records of the first thirty-eight years of government.

After the war, there were three States that had not voted. The Governors of Virginia, South Carolina, and Connecticut were asked to notify their position (House Document NO. 76).

On February 28, 1819, Secretary of State John Quincy Adams reported South Carolina voted no (House Document NO. 129).

On March 10, 1890, the Virginia legislature passed NO. 280 (Virginia Archives Richmond, "misc. file, page 299 for micro-film").

"Be it enacted by the General Assembly, that there shall be published an edition of the Laws of the Commonwealth in which shall be contained the following matters, that is to say, the Constitution of the United States and the amendments thereto..."

This act was the pacific legislated instruction on what was, by law, to be included in the re-publication (a special edition) of the Virginia Civil Code. The Virginia Legislature had already agreed that all Acts were to go into effect on the same day, the day that the Act to re-publish the Civil Code was enacted. Therefore, the "missing lucky" 13th Amendment's official date of ratification would the date of re-publication of the Virginia Civil Code: "March 12, 1819."

Because there were powerful forces against this ratification, extraordinary measures were taken. Four-thousand copies were ordered, the bonded printer Thomas Ritchie was instructed to send a copy to Thomas Jefferson, James Madison, and President James Monroe.

List of Years, States, or Territories Published the "Missing Lucky" 13th Amendment

Colorado	1861, 1862, 1864, 1865, 1866, 1867, 1868
Connecticut	1821, 1824, 1835, 1839
Dakota	1862, 1863, 1867
Florida	1823, 1825, 1838
Georgia	1819, 1822, 1837, 1846
Illinois	1822, 1825, 1827, 1833, 1839
Indiana	1824, 1831, 1838
Iowa	1839, 1842, 1843
Kansas	1855, 1861, 1862, 1868
Kentucky	1822
Louisiana	1825, 1838
Maine	1825, 1831
Massachusetts	1823
Michigan	1827, 1833
Mississippi	1824, 1839
Missouri	1825, 1835, 1840, 1841, 1845
Nebraska	1855, 1856, 1857, 1858, 1859, 1860, 1861, 1862, 1876
North Carolina	1819, 1828
NW Territories	1833
Ohio	1819, 1824, 1831, 1833, 1835, 1848
Pennsylvania	1818, 1824, 1831
Rhode Island	1822
Virginia	1819
Wyoming	1868, 1876

Maine ordered ten-thousand copies of the Constitution with the "missing lucky" 13th Amendment to be printed for use in the schools in 1825 and again in 1831 for their Census edition. Indiana Revised Laws of 1831 published the 13th Article of Amendment on p. 20. The 1867 Colorado Territory edition has the current 13th Amendment freeing the slaves as the 14th Amendment.

Other Publications included The Rights of an American Citizen (1832), The American Politician (1842), and The History of the World (1856).

In 1849 England, the Bank of England and corrupt Americans, who hated the idea that we the people had with the "missing lucky" 13th Amendment the power that could fight corrupt government, was beginning to rise again. The power of the Bar had been suppressed by the "missing lucky" 13th Amendment.

By the time of the War Between the States (it was not a Civil War, there was nothing civil about it) the northern representatives, ignoring the "missing lucky" 13th Amendment, were full of lawyers while the southern representatives had two lawyers, one from Alabama, one from Florida. In 1861 President Lincoln proposed an Amendment. This was the only Amendment that was ever signed by a president. It read "...No Amendment shall be made to the Constitution which will authorize or give to Congress the power to abolish or interfere, within any State, with the domestic institutions thereof, including that of persons held to labor or service by the law of said State."

This Amendment would have permitted slavery and upheld States rights. Illinois was the only one to ratify it.

On April 14, 1865, President Lincoln was assassinated by John Wilkes Booth, an Agent of the Bank of England. A member of the knights of the Golden Circle which was controlled by the bankers.

The Chancellor of Germany, Bismarck said "The death of Lincoln was a disaster for Christendom. There was no man in the United States great enough to wear his boots and the bankers went anew to grab the riches. I fear that foreign bankers with the craftiness and torturous tricks will entirely control the exuberant riches of American and use it to systematically corrupt modern civilization."

On December 6, 1865, the illegal lawyer Congress ratified the new 13th Amendment erasing the true "missing lucky" 13th Amendment which had prohibited "titles of nobility" and "honours" as in Article VI of the Articles of Confederation, and Article I, section 9, clause 8, and Article I, section 10, clause 1 of the United States of America.

Once the "missing lucky" 13th Amendment was suppressed, the money masters and bankers could buy the lawyers. To help disguise this, the International Bar Association in America was changed to the American British Accreditation Registry Association which kept the United States tied to England in all its foreign affairs, and other dealings, and to bankers.

Luke 11:46 – And he said, Woe unto you also, ye lawyers! for ye lade men with burdens grievous to be borne, and ye yourselves touch not the burdens with one of your fingers.

Luke 11:52 – Woe unto you, lawyers! for ye have taken away the key of knowledge: ye entered not in yourselves, and them that were entering in ye hindered.

If everybody in Congress is a member of judicial, isn't this a violation of the separation of powers?

I call this the "missing lucky" 13th Amendment because it makes every law by Congress and the Supreme Court illegal since the 1830's. To have a lawful government we need to vote all the lawyers out of Congress and take back our country from foreign rule, which is the reason the Revolutionary War was fought. Then we would have a government of the people, by the people, and for the people, instead of the special interest groups, by the special interest groups, and for the special interest groups.

The definition of politics: poli means many; tics means bloodsuckers.

The definition of "The Declaration of Independence"

"We hold these truths to be self-evident…" The truths are so obvious that they are immediately apparent to our innate sense of logic and justice.

"…that all men are created equal." This is the foundation of our American legal philosophy of equality for all, under the law.

"that they are endowed by their Creator…" Our rights were endowed by our Creator. They are inborn from God.

"… with certain unalienable rights…" Unalienable: Incapable of being alienated, surrendered, or transferred. Rights: Something to which one has a just or lawful claim. What one fairly has coming… An individual's absolute prerogative to correctness, justice and that which is honorable.

"…that among these (but not limited to) life, liberty, and the pursuit of happiness." These terms are expansive in meaning, as interpreted by the Supreme Court.

"That to secure these rights, governments are instituted among men…" The purpose of government is to secure and protect the rights of people.

"…deriving their just powers from the consent of the governed." The government obtains its power only through the people.

Lawyers are taught in law school that truth is subjective making them professional liars denounced by Jesus. Why you want these people in charge of governing you?

THE ILLEGAL SLAVE AMENDMENT

The 14th Amendment gave every Citizen the right to contract a way their personal and absolute rights. In other words, anyone could give up their absolute rights under the "Bill of Rights" anytime they wanted to by private contract. They could operate outside the Constitution by contract if they wanted to, because it was their law. But by the right of expatriation at any time they could go back to their constitutional government.

The "Civil Rights Act" of 1866 is a private law that only appeared to have jurisdiction over a slave. It's a private law that only affected those who were in contractual relation with the private corporation structure of the United States Government. None of the slaves had any licenses with the United States Government so it was a law that played ignorance because it made them think it did something. It was a law that had few citizens in its jurisdiction. It had only those having licenses or contracts with the United States Government. People in its jurisdiction went from real property law to personal property law outside the protection of common law and the Constitution with its separation of power. Congress made it an Amendment to make it harder for another Congress to repeal it. The 14th Amendment goes against the ideals expressing the Preamble to the Constitution. Congress wanted to nationalize all civil rights to make federal power supreme. This makes the private life of every citizen under them.

The 14th Amendment made individuals a federal citizen of the municipal corporation of Washington, D.C. It made the Senate and House operating for the benefit of private commercial law. Before the 14th Amendment, the Senate functioned for non-commercial public municipal law benefit which is to benefit the individual under republican law and the House functioned for private commercial benefit. It made each person responsible for the public debt by making them beneficiaries of the "public trust".

The 14th Amendment is a private non-positive law because it was enacted to set up a voluntary trust relationship that any citizen could join which shifted the citizenship of each American that joined form being a state citizen to being a citizen of the private corporation of government.

The 14th Amendment moved big business into the public sector to control the people for their assumed benefit which was actually the benefit of the corporations. The price of these benefits is the loss of liberty under the Constitution and common law. As a non-14th Amendment Citizen people could offer their services without interference of civil license authority because there is no jurisdiction over someone who is not a citizen of the 14th Amendment public municipal trust.

With the 14th Amendment private law could be used outside the Constitution to financially enslave the people and destroy the republican union.

The 14th Amendment Sec.1 deals with trust law, as stated "in subject to" which is used in trusts which are private contractual agreements. It makes the people a citizen of the United States first and a citizen of the State second.

The 14th Amendment is private unilateral contract law used to dictate public policy. The part that says "in subject to" means that you have a choice if you want to be "in subject to' or not.

To make the 14th Amendment constitutional, the day before Congress passed it they passed 15 United States Statutes at Large, Ch 249-250, pgs 223-224, Section 1, R.S. 1999, 8 USC 1481 also known as the "Expatriation Statute". This public municipal law can be used for private purposes to remove themselves from the private trust law operating in the public sector. A private individual who is bound by private law promoting public policy of compelled performance which you had no choice in, can use the public positive statue law to go back to the liberty and protection of the Republic and its separation of powers. This is used to get out of any United States Government policy or law, including those of these political subdivisions that are based on private law. This means if you are bound by any compelled performance which you had no choice in you are under jurisdiction of the United States Government and its political subdivisions when there is no republican form of government and its separation of powers. You can break that dictatorial jurisdiction by using Public Laws for your private benefits. The 14th Amendment is a "quasi contractual" which means it is not a common law contract, but an "adhesion" or "unilateral" contract whereas only one party binds them self. A person agrees to the private trust law by their silence. If you do not let your choice be known, the trust will assume you have agreed to be a part of and beneficiary of it. It will be assumed that you have gifted your life for the trusts or benefits.

Under the 14th Amendment, if you do not make your wishes known whether or not you are for or against the trust relationship, it is assumed that you are becoming a beneficiary. As a beneficiary you are operating outside the Constitution and you have only relative rights under the "Bill of Rights."

Under private trust law operating as public policy, you are under the conscience of those that make public policy of the trust for the benefit of its members. Special interests of political action groups influence this. Under the 14th Amendment public trusts majority rules. This is why polls are held to see how the public feels. Under the 14th Amendment public trust the majority or mob rules. If special interests groups can create enough influence, policy can be changed to what they have been promoting.

Beneficiaries of the trust are living under an administrative democracy. There is no separation of powers and private rights are subject to the wheel of the majority of the people. Absolute rights are replaced by relative rights.

U.S. Government Training Manual, No. 2000-25 dated WAR DEPARTMENT, Washington, November 30, 1928.

DEMOCRACY: A government of the masses. Authority derived through mass meeting or any other form of "direct" expression. Results in mobocracy. Attitude toward property is communistic — negating property rights. Attitude toward law is that the will of the majority shall regulate, whether it be based upon deliberation or governed by passion, prejudice, and impulse, without restraint or regard to consequences. Results in demagoguism, license, agitation, discontent, anarchy.

REPUBLIC: Authority is derived through the election by the people of public officials best fitted to represent them. Attitude toward property is respect for laws and individual rights, and a sensible economic procedure. Attitude toward law is the administration of justice in accord with fixed principles and established evidence, with a strict regard to consequences. A greater number of citizens and extent of territory may be brought within its compass. Avoids the dangerous extreme of either tyranny or mobocracy. Results in statesmanship, liberty, reason, justice, contentment, and progress. Is the "standard form" of government throughout the world. A republic is a form of government under a Constitution which provides for the election of (1) an executive and (2) a legislative body, who working together in a representative capacity, have all the power of appointment, all power of legislation, all power to raise revenue and appropriate expenditures, and are required to create (3) a judiciary to pass upon the justice and legality of their governmental acts and to recognize (4) certain inherent individual rights. "Take away any one or more of those four elements and you are drifting into autocracy. Add one or more to those four elements and you are drifting into democracy." — Atwood. - Superior to all others. — Autocracy declares the Divine right of kings; its authority can not be

questioned; its powers are arbitrarily or unjustly administered. Democracy is the "direct" rule of the people and has been repeatedly tried without success. Our Constitutional Fathers, familiar with the strength and weakness of both autocracy and democracy, with fixed principles definitely in mind, defined a representative republican form of government. They "made a very marked distinction between a republic and a democracy and said repeatedly and emphatically that they had founded a republic."

- Madison, in the Federalist, emphasized the fact that this government was a republic and not a democracy, the Constitution makers having considered both an autocracy and a democracy as undesirable forms of government while "a republic promises the cure for which we are seeking."

- "In a democracy the people meet and exercise the government in person. In a republic they assemble and administer it by their respective agents." — Madison.

- "The advantage which a republic has over a democracy consists in the substitution of representatives whose enlightened views and virtuous sentiments render them superior to local prejudices and to schemes of injustice." — Madison.

- The American form of government is the oldest republican form of government in the world, and is exercising a pronounced influence in modifying the governments of other nations. Our Constitution has been copied in whole or in part throughout the earth.

Americans have a choice. You can be part of the political commence under the private law merchant of the 14th Amendment as in Erie Railroad Co. v. Tompkins, 304 U.S. 64 (1938) or you can have total liberty and freedoms of civil commence under the public law merchant as in Swift v. Tyson, 41 U.S. 1 (1842) The courts will uphold your choice but if you are silent, the court will rule you with the private law merchant.

HJR 192 eliminated the fixed standard of gold at thirty-five dollars per troy ounce turning gold into a commodity. Since gold had no fixed standard it could fluctuate according to supply and demand effecting real property causing inflation.

The people could have stopped this from happening by making their legal declaration to be involved with private law for public purposes under the 14th Amendment. But because the people did not know how to challenge the 14th Amendment, the people became victims of it.

As a 14th Amendment citizen, the IRS and State Tax Boards are the trustees of your estate. To go back to the republican form of law you used the state probate court to severe your trust relationship and exercising your private use of public municipal law.

The Constitution spells out everything about its operation and relationship to its Citizens. It was designed to be a republic because it protects the minority from the majority which is the opposite of a democracy. The reason all other republics mainly fail is because they do not have an instrument that defines what a republic is and how it should operate.

Before the 14th Amendment, federal district courts had no jurisdiction to deal with in the private individual because they only handled admiralty-maritime law. Only circuit courts and the Supreme Court of the United States operating in the United States Government could have jurisdiction over matters involving citizens from different states. The state courts handled federal questions because they were the courts of original jurisdiction involving contracts. After the 14th Amendment, the United States district courts had jurisdiction in private matters of people involved in the trust because people of the trust now came under admiralty-maritime law outside the Constitution.

The reason people lose their property rights is because 14th Amendment citizens only have equitable interests in property. Under equitable interests you can't prove superior title to access the land as a Citizen of the soil which is a non-14th Amendment Citizen. It is your standing in law that determines your access to the Law to save your land. It's not determined by the title to the land as all land titles in the United States of America are allodial titles. The 14th Amendment jurisdiction deals only with the person in relation to his interest in the land. A commercial system cannot create credit against the substance of the common law-land. It is only created through the person under the 14th Amendment. In the Declaration of Independence real property is not listed as "unalienable" right because real property was the absolute substance that made an individual sovereign in America. It was common law. Under the 14th Amendment the people's property is reclassified as an alienable right which means they have been sold into the slavery of the trust. Therefore, you cannot own property in the absolute sense.

When going to court, usually the lower court Judges do not know about public municipal law for private purposes or the separation of power principles. The way to get due process is in an Appeal to the appellate courts. There are two floors to the Supreme Court Building. The second floor is for a higher law which is a constitutional issue. The Supreme Court has to hear all constitution cases. A 14th Amendment citizen can't be heard at that level of law because they voluntarily gave up that right and are operating at law outside the Constitution.

To become a non-14th Amendment Citizen, publish a Legal Notice one or more times depending on your states Statue. It is alright if your newspaper puts this declaration under Public Notice. Start the process severing the Trust by filing a Declaration of Independence. After it's been filed and advertised in the newspaper, you should send back an Affidavit of Publication to be used as an "Exhibit" for evidence to the probate court of your will.

Declaration of Independence

I, _____ in the name of the Almighty Creator, By my Declaration of Independence solemnly Publish and Declare my Right to expatriate absolute, my res in trust to the foreign jurisdiction known as the municipal corporation of the District of Columbia, a democracy, and return to the Republic. Any and all past and present political ties implied by operation of law or otherwise in trust with the democracy is hereby dissolved. I, _____ have full power to contract, establish commerce as guaranteed by the full 10 Amendments to the Bill of Rights to the Constitution of the united Stated of America, a Republic.

Done this _____ day of _____, 20_____.

Signed, _____

Address _____

Notary _____

Done this _____ day of _____, 20_____.

Notary Public Seal

If the majority of the people (more than 50%) did this, money would have to be backed by gold and silver.

You cannot use precedent law because each case is individual and separate and based on Statue and case law. License lawyers can't help you because they are licensed to practice in private commercial law functioning in Article I courts at law.

The Attorney General's office may be housed with the tax collection and enforcing agencies because they handle private law for public commercial purposes. This is why all attorneys have the title "attorney at law". They are licensed to practice private law for public commercial purposes.

Only the individual as a non-14th Amendment Citizen can be an "attorney in-law" because you, as the govern, control the law when in the Republic. You have control over the grant that authorizes those who have the privilege to use private "at law" and its equity for public commercial purposes.

"In law" is to function where the courts reveal your position in the Law which is using your unalienable rights under the Constitution.

"At law" is the function where the courts rule the Law is the will of the legislation in trust with the person. It is restrictive because if operates outside the Constitution. So the individual, as a Citizen of the Republic, has the power to destroy private commercial law ventures that are being misused for public commercial purposes to their detriment.

It is everyone's duty and obligation under the Declaration of Independence to challenge unjust private law, such as unjust commercial policy that violates liberty. In the Republic the individual rules, not the majority. The Constitution is to protect the minority from the majority because it provides for the individual to use public law to protect their beliefs from the majority.

14th Amendment person:	vs.	Non-14th Amendment individual:
- American flag with gold fringe, supports the ten planks of communism, the flag most Americans serve under		- American flag, without gold fringe, so long as you don't infringe on someone else's rights, gives you all the rights of a King and that's a lot of rights, the flag you pledge allegiance to
- You're just another brick in the wall.		- You are the wall.
- You can't have any pudding unless you eat your meat.		- You can have your pudding without eating your meat, which works out really good for vegetarians.
- Black market thrives		- No black market
- Relative property rights		- Absolute property rights
- Compelled performance, guilty until proven innocent		- True liberty to volunteer, innocent until proven guilty
- Social Security; Anyone giving up God given rights for security deserves to lose both.		- Develop own security
- All government aid		- Pursue interests without interference
- Government supervision		- Develop own standards
- Indirect Taxes		- Direct tax
- Licenses		- Full right to contract with anyone for anything without licenses
- Code Pleading		- Statutes at Large
- At law		- In law
- Article I Courts or Territorial Courts – referred to as Legislative or Ecclesiastical Courts		- Article III Courts of judicial Power in Law and Equity
- Law of sea – limited liability in maritime venture for payment of debt		- Law of land – Negotiable Instrument Law – all debt must be paid

- Revised Statutes are private national law for public purposes "in rem." Rem acts on the "res" for "the thing."

- Statutes are public municipal law to be used for private purposes – acts on person (in personam)

- de facto government (outside Constitution) Art. I, Sec. 8 Cl. 17

- de jure government (inside Constitution)

- Local Law – sustained by "Erie RR v. Tomkins"

- General Law – sustained by "Swift v. Tyson"

- Uniform Commercial Code - Private Merchant use inflation to fund growth – False production. No fixed Standard

- Gold Standard – Public Law Merchant uses no inflation – true productivity is key. Prices at par value

- Unilateral Contracts – where there is a silent third party involved in compelling performance. Trust Law.

- Bilateral Contracts – where there is a meeting of the minds. Two party transaction. No compelled performance.

- Roman Civil Law   Admiralty-Maritime Privilege

Common Civil Law

- Relative Rights to self and property. Substance of private law is the conscience of trust.

- Absolute Rights and title to self and property. Substance of Public Law is the rights of man.

- Operates under Art. I Sec. 8, Cl. 4 – (can interfere with estate under private "implied" contracts)

- Operates under Art. IV, Sec. 4 (cannot interfere with estate)

- Individual considered commercial person or "goods in commerce" for servicing public debt. Also referred to by state as "human resource."

- Private individual

- Freedom of conscience as long as it agrees with the majority or the masses.

- Freedom of conscience of individual, beholding to no one.

- "several states of the union"

- "states in this union"

- "a" territory

- "the" territory

- No separation of powers (no separation of church and state)

- Separation of Powers (separation of church and state)

- Confederacy under Articles of Confederation and N.W. Ordinance.

- No communal relationship

- Indirect Taxes

- Direct Taxes

- All courts take jurisdiction through the 14th Amendment until one proves otherwise. Codes are streamlined private interpretation of statutes at large for public purpose. Codes allow the courts to take judicial notice of 14th Amendment. Codes apply to anyone who has not made a public notice of his political choice (Will) by declaration.

- 15 Statue at Large is designed to keep federal courts from taking jurisdiction. Courts cannot take judicial notice of 14th Amendment.

- Unisex No individualism

- Doctrine of compliments Special individualism

- Guilty until proven innocent. Burden of proof rest with the accused. If you disagree with this, try pleading innocent. If you are found not guilty it does not mean that you are innocent, it means that they could not prove you did the crime.

- Innocent until proven guilty. Burden of proof rests with the accuser.

- Res judicata – judgment bases on merits of case and legal precedence. Courts tell what the intent of legislation. Issue already decided, have no legal recourse.

- Plead to the Law or Statute for defense. Law awards damages and Equity on this side. Compels performance of award.

- Twilight Zone, Quasi Law. No time and place. Only exist in abstract space. Artificial-abstract false and theoretical, conscience, changeable.

- Fixed in place and time as in permanent domicile or resident. Real-substance matter and content. Heart-Soul-Spirit

- No initiative and no true production.

- Individual incentive and true production.

- Erie Railroad v. Tompkins 1938. Individual subject to the political commerce under the private law merchant.

- Swift v. Tyson 1842. Individual subject to the civil commerce under the public law merchant.

- Public Social Security Trust. Marine Insurance for limited liability required under international law - individual is considered common carrier – all carriers must have insurance to cover costs of involvement in joint venture for profit (a debt never paid.) "A case in admiralty does not, in fact, arise under the Constitution or laws of the United States." American Ins. Co. v. Canter, 1 Pet. 511, 545 (1828).

- Negotiable Instrument Law No limited liability interference. All debt must be paid. Clearfield Trust Co. v. United States, 318 U.S. 363; 63 S.Ct. 573.

- High overhead

- Low overhead

- Living in the State of _____ Same area, different jurisdiction

- Living in _____ State Same area, different jurisdiction

- All business and trade over-seen. Regulated by third party administrative trust who take a piece of the action.

- No third party intervention. Article I, Section 10 in full force for individual, i.e., State cannot interfere in obligation of contract. The State of the District of Columbia,. D.C is considered a state in international law. See Geoffrey v. U.S., 133 U.S. 258; 105 S.Ct. 295.

- Private Enterprise Choices based on what agencies administrative rules/codes allow.

- Free Enterprise Liberty of choice in all areas of life without government interference.

- "New World Order" actually administrative democracy based on Old World Order

- Republican government guaranteed to the states as per Art. IV, Sect. 4.

American Ins. Co. et al., The v. Canter (356 Bales of Cotton), 1 Pet. 511, 545 (1828)
"A case in admiralty does not, in face, arise under the Constitution or Laws of the United States."

Clearfield Trust Co. v. United States, 318 U.S. 363; 63 S.Ct. 573 (Mar. 1, 1943)
"The rights and duties of the United States on commercial paper which it issues are governed by federal law rather than local law."

"In absence of an applicable act of Congress fixing rights and duties of the United States on commercial paper which is issues, it is for the federal courts to fashion the governing rule of law according to their own standards."

"The federal law merchant developed under the regime of Swift v. Tyson represented general commercial law rather than a choice of a federal rule designed to protect a federal right, but it stands as a convenient source of reference for regarding rights and duties of the United States on commercial paper which it issues.

"The United States as drawee of commercial paper stands in no different lights than any other drawee."

Geoffrey v. U.S. 258; 105 S.Ct. 295

The District of Columbia is considered a state in international law.

Black's Law Dictionary – Sixth Edition:

Person – Aliens – Aliens are "persons" within meaning of 14th Amendment and are thus protected by equal protection clause against discriminatory state action. Foley v. Connelie, D.C.N.Y., 419 F.Supp. 889, 891.

Alien – A foreign born person who has not qualified as a citizen of the country; but an alien is a person within the meaning of the 14th Amendment due process clause of the U.S. Constitution to same extent as a citizen. Galvan v. Press, 347 U.S. 522, 74 S.Ct. 737, 742, 98 L.Ed. 911.

By this definition, it seems that anyone who is in the United States, rather born in the United States or not, is a citizen under the 14th Amendment. Therefore there are no illegal aliens.

Unalienable – Inalienable; Incapable of being aliened, that is, sold or transferred.

By this definition, you cannot give up an unalienable right, which makes this another way the 14th Amendment is illegal.

There is some question as the legality of the ratification of the 14th Amendment, being that corrupt carpetbaggers and the military forced voters to ratify it. They did this by literally putting guns to their heads.

Can you say corruption, boys and girls? – Mr. Rogers

"Freedom is the emancipation from arbitrary rule of other men." – Mortimer Adler

"The sole object and only legitimate end of government is to protect the Citizen in the enjoyment of life, liberty, and property, and when government assumes other functions it is usurpation and oppression." – Alabama Constitution; Article I §35

"Liberty is one of the most precious gifts which heaven has bestowed on man; with it we cannot compare the treasures which the earth contains or the sea conceals; for liberty, as for honor, we can and ought to risk our lives; and, on the other hand, captivity is the greatest evil that can befall man." – Miguel De Cervantes

"The price of freedom is eternal vigilance…Never trust your government. You need a revolution every twenty years, just to keep the government honest!" – Thomas Jefferson

WALKING THE PLANKS

On May 1, 1776 a secret society called the Illuminati was created by German professor Adrian Weishaupt. He infiltrated the Continental Order of Free Masons creating the illuminated Free Masonary. The New World Order is based upon Communism and Socialism. The principles were no God, no religion, and a hand picked few to rule all the world. The Illuminati were backers of the Bolshevick Revolution. Karl Marx set up a heavy progressive and graduated an income tax system saying "to crush the middle class under the disguise of a need to finance the government." Marx also stated in 1872 "a social revolution or an economic conquest could be accomplished by peaceful means in America by taking advantage of libertarian traditions and free institution to subvert them."

TEN PLANKS OF THE COMMUNIST MANIFESTO

1. ABOLITION OF PROPERTY IN LAND AND THE APPLICATION OF ALL RENTS OF LAND TO PUBLIC PURPOSES. (Zoning – Model ordinances proposed by Secretary of Commerce Herbert Hoover. If you think you own your land, don't pay your rent (property tax) and you will see who owns it.)

2. A HEAVY PROGRESSIVE OR GRADUATED INCOME TAX. (Corporate Tax Act of 1909, The Revenue Act of 1913, section 2, Income Tax)

3. ABOLITION OF ALL RIGHTS OF INHERITANCE. (Partially accomplished by enactment of various State and Federal "estate tax" laws as in Inheritance Taxes and Reform Probate Laws.)

4. CONFISCATION OF THE PROPERTY OF ALL EMIGRANTS AND REBELS. (Frequently accomplished by prosecuting "rebels" of government policies on charges of violations of non-existing administrative or regulatory laws. Sedition Act of 1798; I.R.S. powers; Executive order 11490, Sec. 2002, - giving total power over all personal property to the General Services Administration.)

5. CENTRALIZATION OF CREDIT IN THE HANDS OF THE STATE, BY MEANS OF A NATIONAL BANK WITH STATE CAPITAL AND AN EXCLUSIVE MONOPOLY. (The Federal Reserve System (the Federal Reserve Act of 1913) unlawfully delegated the power to regulate the value of our money to the Federal Reserve, which is a private corporation. See U.S. Constitution, Art. 1, Sec. 8 (5) – only Congress can have this power.)

6. CENTRALIZATION OF THE MEANS OF COMMUNICATION AND TRANSPORTATION IN THE HANDS OF THE STATE. (Federal Radio Commission, Federal Communications Commission, Air Commerce Act, Civil Aeronautics Act, Federal Aviation Administration, Federal Highway Act of 1916, et. al. FCC regulations and Executive order 10995 provides for the takeover of all communications media; State Drivers Licenses provide for State regulation of the "privilege" to travel; D.O.T. regulations and Executive Order 10999 provide for the takeover of all modes of transportation.)

7. EXTENSION OF FACTORIES AND INSTRUMENTS OF PRODUCTION OWNED BY THE STATE, THE BRINGING INTO CULTIVATION OF WASTE LANDS, AND THE IMPROVEMENT OF THE SOIL GENERALLY IN ACCORDANCE WITH A COMMON

PLAN. (The Federal Government has total production and labor control under Executive Order 11490 through the Departments of Labor, Commerce, Agriculture, and Interior. Dep't. of Interior controls Bureau of Land Management, Bureau of Reclamation, Fish & Wildlife Service, etc.)

8. EQUAL LIABILITY OF ALL TO LABOR, ESTABLISHMENT OF INDUSTRIAL ARMIES ESPECIALLY FOR AGRICULTURE. (American Federation of Labor, Interstate Commerce Act, Department of Labor, Civil Works Administration, Fair Labor Standards Act of 1938, et. al. Federal Emergency Public Works Programs; Executive Order 11000 provides for forced mobilization of civilians into work brigades.)

9. COMBINATION OF AGRICULTURE WITH MANUFACTURING INDUSTRIES, GRADUAL ABOLITION OF THE DISTINCTION BETWEEN TOWN AND COUNTRY, BY A MORE EQUITABLE DISTRIBUTION OF POPULATION OVER THE COUNTRY. (Food processing companies with the cooperation of the Farmers Home Administration buying up farms and creating conglomerates. Using the Re-organization Act of 1949, executive Order 11647, Public Law 89-136, and Executive Order 11731, we will no longer have 50 states with cities and towns, but instead have 10 regions and their respective capitals.)

10. FREE EDUCATION FOR ALL CHILDREN IN PUBLIC SCHOOL. ABOLITION OF CHILDREN'S FACTORY LABOR IN ITS PRESENT FORM. COMBINATION OF EDUCATION WITH INDUSTRIAL PRODUCTION. (Smith-Hughes Act of 1917, National School Lunch Act of 1946, National Defense Education Act of 1958, et. al. Free state public schools; child abuse laws; child labor laws where children work with State approval; abolition of private apprenticeships and the creation of state controlled apprenticeships as in the Fair Labor Standards Act of 1937.)

Are you a communist? Are you aware that 14th Amendment citizens support communism? We have met the enemy and he is us.

"We will bury you from within." – Nikita Khrushchev

Bow down to those you want to serve, you're going to get what you deserve. Everything that happens to you is your own fault.

"God grants liberty only to those who love it and are always ready to guard and defend it." Daniel Webster

"Perfect freedom is as necessary to the health and vigor of commerce as it is to the health and vigor of citizenship." Patrick Henry

"If a nation expects to be ignorant and free it expects something that can not be." Thomas Jefferson

DEMON RATS

You dirty demon rats karma is going to get you – James Cagney

Democracy is the recurrent suspicion that more than half of the people are right more than half of the time. It is two wolves and a sheep deciding what's for dinner (mob rule). Throughout history, it lasts no more than 200 years and ends up in a dictatorship or revolution. America started going into a democracy by 1840. It is in violation of Article IV, Section 4 of the Constitution of the United States: "The United States shall guarantee to every State in this Union a Republican Form of Government…" Democracy was a curse word to the Founding Fathers. It is mentioned zero times in the United States Constitution, the Supreme Law of the land. It does not work because right is right no matter if everybody says it's wrong and wrong is wrong no matter if everybody says it's right. You can't escape karma. It must be balanced with dharma. Payback is hell.

Patrick Henry did not say "Give me a democracy or give me death." Democracy is simply in deterioration of the Republic. Since America's Constitution was established, in 200 years France has gone through 7 governments, Italy has gone through 51.

Founding Father Fisher Ames said, "A democracy is a volcano which conceals the firing materials of it's own destruction. These will produce an eruption and carry desolation in the way."

Founding Father Benjamin Rush said, "A simple democracy is the devils own government."

Founding Father John Adams said, "Remember, democracy never lasts long. It soon wastes exhausts and murders itself. There never was a democracy that did not commit suicide."

During the Constitutional Convention of 1787 in the records of James McHenry of Maryland, a lady named Mrs. Powel asked Benjamin Franklin, "What kind of government have you delegates given us?" He said, "A Republic, Madame, if you can keep it." Also, Elbridge Gerry of Massachusetts said, "The evils we experience flow from the excessive democracy."

THE TRUTH ABOUT SLAVERY

Slavery wasn't invented in America. It had been around for thousands of years. People who were captured had to do work for clothing and food. To the victor goes the spoils.

The Spanish enslaved Native Americans to haul their goods. The Dutch in 1619 imported twenty slaves from Africa to work in Virginia tobacco farms. They were indentured laborers, treated the same as indentured servants.

In the early years, many people became indentured servants for four to seven years. At the end of their servitude they were suppose to get land, a bushel of corn, tools, and a new suit of clothes. The servitude was done in hope that the servants would die before the end of the servitude. They had to give away a lot of land to those who survived. The greedy bankers and plantation owners wanted people who would work for nothing. Indentured servants and indentured laborers had to be paid at the end of the servitude, but the slaves did not. Plus, the slaves' offspring would provide a workforce forever. However, the first African slaves got their freedom at the end of their indentured servitude. Some even became slaved owners. The three biggest slave owners were Africans. The first slave owner in Virginia was an African named Freeman who got his land by indentured servitude.

The African slave trade was started by the Portuguese and their African allies, who wanted to get rid of their rival tribes. The Portuguese built a fort called the Mine on the African Gold Coast and packed it with thousands of people between the ages of fifteen and twenty-five. In four-hundred years, twenty million people passed through these slave forts.

England traded merchandise for African slaves, which were traded to the English colonies in the West Indies for merchandise such as sugar, tobacco, rice, potatoes, tomatoes, and rum that the slave labor had produced. This was done under the approval of the King of England and Parliament. In 1772 Benjamin Franklin wrote in "The Somerset Case and the Slave Trade" that one of Britain's great sins against America was forcing slavery on it.

In the beginning, there were slaves in the north. In 1760 Philadelphia's population was 10% slaves. The northern farmers didn't need slaves because their farms were small, but the northern merchants thrived on slavery. As southern plantations got bigger, the demand for slavery grew. It was economics.

Everyone wants to blame the white southerners for slavery in America. The blame should be on the bankers, plantation owners, the 126 slave ships owned by the merchants, the African tribes that captured and sold the slaves, the King of England, and Parliament. Slave owners were a minority in the south. When Virginia gave up the Ohio Valley Territory, its only stipulation was that it could not have slavery. After the War Between the States, it was the north who wanted the slaves to be counted as three fifths of a person.

The Constitution specified the importation of slaves was to be halted by 1808, but by that time, they had enough slaves and didn't need to import anymore.

The 1790 Census reported 697,897 slaves out of 4 million people. There were 47, 664 families out of 410,636 that owned slaves, a ratio close to 1 out of 9. The 1810 Census reported 1,191,354 slaves, which was an increase of 70% in two decades.

The definition of the N word is slave. This means everybody with a Social Security number is an N word. The Founding Fathers thought that anybody giving up rights for security deserves to lose both. Johann W. von Goethe said, "None are more hopelessly enslaved than those who falsely believe they are free!"

14th Amendment, Section 1: All persons born or naturalized in the United States, and subject to the jurisdiction thereof, are citizens of the United States and of the State wherein they reside. No State shall make or enforce any law which shall abridge the privileges or immunities of citizens of the United States; not shall any State deprive any person of life, liberty, or property, without due process of law; nor deny to any person within its jurisdiction the equal protection of the laws.

There was no such thing as a United States citizen before the 14th Amendment. Everyone was a Citizen of the United States of America, a Natural Born Citizen, and a Citizen of the United States, a Citizen of several States, American National, or a Citizen of the American Republic.

"The persons declared to be citizens are "All persons born are naturalized in these United States and subject to the jurisdiction thereof." The evident meaning of these last words is not merely subject in some respect or degree to the jurisdiction of the United States, but completely subject..." Elk v. Wilkins, 112 U.S. 94, 101 102 1884

Subject to liable, subordinate, subservient, inferior, obedient; govern or affected by; provided that; provided; answerable for. Homan v. Employers Reinsurance Corporation, 345 Mo. 650, 136 S.W. 2d 289, 302

Sovereign: A person, body, or state in which independent a supreme authority is vested; a chief ruler with supreme power; a king or other ruler in a monarchy. Black's Law Dictionary 6th Edition

A natural born citizen of the 50 states already had sovereign Citizenship as in Article II, Sec. 1, Clause 15 of the Constitution.

The Creator has superior rights to what was created. The 14th Amendment created a subject citizen. When you become a 14th Amendment citizen, you are giving up rights for privileges. You hold your citizenship in a bankrupt corporation called the United States. You reside, not inhabit. Few people fit this jurisdiction, but you can join up by voluntary servitude when you get a government contract like Social Security, licenses, government job, food stamps, welfare, military, etc. You go from a sovereign who has all the rights of a King, which means you can do anything you want so long as you don't infringe on anyone else's rights, to a subject citizen. Sovereign Citizens do not pay income or property taxes. The only taxes they pay are sales tax, which is a direct tax. You don't need business licenses or permits. There are no building codes or zoning regulations.

You don't hear about sovereign Citizens because Congress has no jurisdiction over them. They are not in the titles of the U.S. Code. The reason it is not taught in public schools is because it would be bad business for the government if the people were to know that they were giving up the rights of a King.

According to the U.S. Constitution, Article I, Section 8, Para. 17, Congress shall have exclusive jurisdiction over the District of Columbia, Federal possessions, and territories. Exclusive means that there is no other power within that area.

Federal Rules of Criminal Procedure, Rule 54 (c) - Act of Congress includes an act of Congress locally applicable to and in force in the District of Columbia, in Puerto Rico, in a territory or in an insular possession...

Only the States have jurisdiction in criminal and civil matters. 18 USC, Sec. 7 (3) Any lands reserved or acquired for the use of the United States, and under the exclusive or concurrent jurisdiction thereof, or any place purchased or otherwise acquired by the United States by consent of the legislature of the State in which the same shall be, for the erection of a fort, magazine, arsenal, dockyard, or other needful building.

The Federal Government jurisdiction is just on the property of the United States like Post Offices and military bases or high seas.

Under your birth right, if there is not victim there is no crime. If there is no crime there is no jurisdiction. No governments have jurisdiction over a sovereign inhabitant of a State unless there is a crime committed and to have a crime, there must be an injured party.

The United States Constitution is a contract subject to Article I, Sec. 8. Outside of that, Congress cannot legislate Public Law in the united 50 States. When you take an oath to uphold the Constitution, you have entered into a contract and become the servant of the sovereign.

When Alexander Hamilton wanted to make the President a near monarch for life, Benjamin Franklin noted, "A person's life sometimes lasted longer than his mental or physical capabilities." He wanted the President to return to the role of an average Citizen after his term arguing that "returning to the mass of the people was degrading was contrary to the republic principles. In free Governments, the rulers are the servants, and the people are their superiors and sovereigns. For the former therefore to return among the latter was not to degrade but to promote them." You can protect your rights by putting "Without Prejudice" UCC 1-207 meaning that you are reserving all rights and that you do not have to perform a contract unless you know all the facts you entered into. In other words, you are doing it under protest.

GIVE ME BACK MY BULLETS

Defenseless people rounded up and exterminated in the 20th Century because of gun control: 56 million.

In 1911, Turkey established gun control. From 1915 to 1917, 1.5 million Armenians, unable to defend themselves, were rounded up and exterminated.

In 1929, the Soviet Union established gun control. From 1929 to 1953, about 20 million dissidents, unable to defend themselves, were rounded up and exterminated.

China established gun control in 1935. From 1948 to 1952, some 20 million political dissidents, unable to defend themselves, were rounded up and exterminated.

Germany established gun control in 1938 and from 1939 to 1945, a total of 13 million Jews and others who were unable to defend themselves were rounded up and exterminated.

Cambodia established gun control in 1956. From 1975 to 1977, one million "educated" people, unable to defend themselves, were rounded up and exterminated.

Guatemala established gun control in 1964. From 1964 to 1981, some 100,000 Mayan Indians, unable to defend themselves, were rounded up and exterminated.

Uganda established gun control in 1970. From 1971 to 1979, 300,000 Christians, unable to defend themselves, were rounded up and exterminated.

For the first year since gun owners in Australia were forced by a new law to surrender 640,381 personal firearms to be destroyed by their own government, costing Australia taxpayers more than $500 million dollars, homicides were up 3.2 percent, assaults were up 8.6 percent, and armed robberies were up 44 percent.

In the state of Victoria alone, homicides with firearms were up 300 percent. Note that while the law-abiding citizens turned them in, the criminals did not, and criminals still possess their guns.

The previous 25 years showed a steady decrease in armed robbery with firearms. This has changed drastically upward since criminals now are guaranteed that their prey is unarmed.

There has also been a dramatic increase in break-ins and assaults of the elderly. Australian politicians are at loss to explain how public safety has decreased, after such monumental effort and expense was expended in successfully ridding Australian society of guns. The Australian experience and the other historical facts about prove it.

You won't see this data on the news. Guns in the hands of honest citizens save lives and property and, yes, gun-control laws adversely affect only the law-abiding citizens.

The next time someone talks in favor of gun control, please remind him of this history lesson. With Guns, we are Citizens. Without them, we are Subjects.

During World War II the Japanese decided not to invade American because they knew most Americans were armed.

Admiral Yamamoto who crafted the attack on Pearl Harbor had attended Harvard University from 1919 - 1921 and was Naval Attaché to the United States from 1925 – 1928. Most of our Navy was destroyed at Pearl Harbor and our Army had been deprived of funding and was ill prepared to defend the country.

It was reported that when asked why Japan did not follow up the Pearl Harbor attack with an invasion of the United States Mainland, his reply was that he had lived in the United States and knew that almost all households had guns.

The 2nd Amendment keeps the government from taking away our God given right to bear arms. Without the 2nd Amendment, we would not have any other amendments. It is an unalienable right.

The US Government intends to force gun control and a complete ban on all weapons for US citizens through the signing of international treaties with foreign nations. Once the US Government signs these international treaties, all US citizens will be subject to those gun laws created by foreign governments.

2nd Amendment – A well regulated Militia, being necessary to the security of a free State, the right of the people to keep and bear Arms, shall not be infringed.

What part of "shall not be infringed" does the US Government not understand?

The definition of infringe: To break or disregard the terms of; violate - to infringe on (or upon) to transgress or trespass on rights or privileges; encroach, to infringe on liberty. By this definition it seems the right to keep and bear arms cannot be taken away from you, and you cannot give it up even if you wanted to.

THE FORGOTTEN NINTH AMENDMENT

IX – The enumeration in the Constitution of certain rights shall not be construed to deny or disparage others retained by the people.

These other rights are called unenumerated rights which is defined as rights not specifically listed in the Constitution. Examples:

Abortion – The reason you shouldn't get an abortion isn't because of what government says. It is because beings of love do not assassinate unborn children. If you cannot handle this mentally, you may turn to drugs and alcohol for escape until you can forgive yourself. If everybody for abortions was aborted, there would be no more abortions.

Government Protection – Blackstone defined as a right consisting of "a persons legal and uninterrupted enjoyment of his life, his limbs, his body, his health and his reputation. Magna Charta states everyone has the right to "security of person."

Marriage – Years ago, the only people who needed a marriage license were Interracial. This was illegal because statues prohibiting marriage between persons of different races have been held to be invalid as contrary to equal protection clause of the Constitution. Loving v. Virginia, 388 U.S. 1, 87 S. Ct. 1817, 18 L. Ed. 2d. 1010 "No State shall… pass any… Laws impairing the Obligations of Contracts…." Article I, Sec. 10 Para. 1 U.S Constitution. "A state may not impose a charge for the enjoyment of a right granted by the Federal Constitution." Murdock v. Pennsylvania 319 U.S. 105, 113 (1943) People needlessly get marriage licenses because they think it's the Law. Why are you involving `the government in a contract between you, your spouse, and God? Churches marry people to the State and pledge their congregation to them by filing a Corp. 501-C3. When government got involved, divorces went up. When you get married with a license, your children become wards of the state. The definition of marriage in Black's Law Dictionary, sixth edition, says it's a legal union of one man and one woman as husband and wife. Singer v. Hara 11 Wash. App. 247, 522 P.2d 1187 (1974) By this definition, same sex marriages are illegal. Marriage, as distinguished from the agreement to marry and from the act of becoming married, is the legal status, condition, or relation of one man and one woman united in law for life, or until divorced, for the discharge of each other and the community of the duties illegally incumbent on those whose association is founded on the distinction of sex. A contract, according to the form described by law, by which a man and a woman capable of entering into such contract, mutually engage with each other to live their whole lives (or until divorced) together in state of union which ought to exist between a husband and wife. The word also signifies the act, ceremony, or formal proceeding by which persons take each other for husband and wife. A prenuptial agreement is a common law contract. You can put whatever you want in it. Since the divorce rate is 50%, you may save a lot of money in lawyer's fees. In case of a divorce with children, the woman gets the bulk of the property so they don't become a burden to the State. Under common law, unless stated otherwise, the man is in charge of the estate and what it produces, and the woman is in charge of the household.

Termination of Life – Right to refuse medical help. To be taken off life support.

Other examples – Education & Privacy

ENEMY OF THE PEOPLE

"We the people are the rightful masters, both of Congress and the Courts, not to overthrow the Constitution, but to overthrow the men who pervert the Constitution."

– Abraham Lincoln.

In 1933 the Unites States declared bankruptcy. This is in the United States Code and there is other evidence in treaty modifications, Executive Orders, Congressional Records, and the absence on lawful money. The Gold Reserve Act of 1933 made it illegal to own gold other than jewelry or rare coins. The Gold Reserve went to the Federal Banks as part of US obligations.

The 1935 D series Silver Certificates were changed to read "legal tender for all debts public and private". A Silver Dollar was now a Dollar in Silver, changing the meaning of a Dollar from precise grains of Silver as in the Coinage Act of 1792 to a floating commodity.

The Securities and Exchange Act of 1933 changed the collateral requirements to Federal Reserve Notes and Silver Certificates creating a monopoly for the Federal Reserve System.

The Treasury Department has stated that Federal Reserve Notes are not Dollars but are Insurance Scrip. This changed the Dollar symbol from a "U" over struck with an "S" to an "I" over the "S". This is the accounting symbol on the Mexican Peso and no accuracies linking it to the International Monetary Fund.

In 1972 Nixon demonetized silver. This changed the debt to be back by nothing and cause 9 years of inflation, destroying the wealth of Americans. This also increased taxes without increasing buying power.

Five generations of family wealth was destroyed in one decade. Leaving the biggest debt in American History to the next generation.

Senate Report 93-549 (1973) states:

"Since March 9, 1933, the United States has been in a state of national emergency. A majority of the people of the United States have lived their lives under emergency rule. For 40 years freedoms and governmental procedures, guaranteed by the constitution have, in varying degrees, been abridged by laws brought forth by states of national emergency..."

"These hundreds of statutes delegate to the president extraordinary powers, ordinarily exercised by Congress, which affect the lives of American Citizens in a host of all-encompassing manners. This vast range of powers, taken together, confers enough authority to rule this country without reference to normal constitutional process."

"Under the powers delegated by these statutes the President may seize property, organize and control the means of production; seize commodities [i.e. The People's gold, silver and currency] assign military forces abroad; institute martial law; seize and control all transportation and communication, regulate the operation of private enterprise, restrict travel, and in a multitude of particular ways, control the lives of all American citizens."

Horn vs. The Fed of Minneapolis (1968) – US citizens lack the standing to challenge the constitutionality of the Federal Reserve because the War and Emergency Powers Act of 1933 stated that "We the People" became the enemy of the US Government. FDR committed treason when he suspended the US Constitution and made the people the enemy of the US Government.

The 16th Amendment did not give Congress the right to charge an income tax. It did not empower any new taxation on the people by Congress. According to the Constitution, taxation should be equal throughout the states. There is no law that compels you to file a tax return unless you manufacture or sell alcohol, tobacco, or firearms. It is your right to challenge what is and is not constitutional. If the IRS tells you different, ask them where in Title 26 does it say you have to file? You can file an order to show cause. The IRS may file a federal tax lien under sections 6321, 6322, and 6323 of the IR Codes. Title 26 is an excise tax for the ATF. An excise tax is levied on the manufacture sale or consumption alcohol, tobacco, and firearms. The IRS liens are through the ATF. If the IRS agents file a lien you can sue the agents for extortion and fraud. To pay an excise tax is not an income tax. The IRS operates under the ATF. Title 27 is the law that triggers Title 26. The 16th Amendment was never properly ratified. It needed 35 states to ratify it and only got 29.

In the IRS Handbook for Special Agents OP the front cover states it is not for the public. "AGENTS… Our tax system is based on individual self assessment and voluntary compliance… the material contained in this handbook is confidential in character. It must not under any circumstances be made available to persons outside the service."

President Barack Obama has issued an executive order apologizing to Great Britain for America's Declaration of Independence in 1776. "It's time to move away from the failed policies of the past," said Obama during a Rose Garden Press Conference, "and the first step is apologizing for the original sin of this nation against the sensibilities of the international community. The Declaration of Independence from the wise and the benevolent guiding hand of Great Britain was, in the eyes of some, an important step, but the manner in which it was handled was an affront to acceptable diplomatic norms…" "Therefore," declared Obama, "We the People of the United States of America, do formally apologize and ask for the forgiveness of the descendants and heirs of Great Britain's people in monarchy." He apologized to the country that brought slavery and War to America.

Other Court Cases:
  Silent Weapons for Quiet Wars – Declaration of War upon the American people.
  Public Law 87-297 (1961) – Disarmament of U.S. Military/surrender to U.N.
  Young v. U.S. – Acts of War upon the people
  World Heritage Treaty – All land in America, except Allodial Title land, was traded away for debt.
  Executive Order 11649 – Statehood Abolished

Benjamin Franklin designed most of the Great Seal. His proposal was to have E Pluribus Unum on the front and Pharaoh being engulfed by the Red Sea with the quote, "Rebellion to Tyrants is obedience to God."

"If we could just send the same bunch of men to Washington for the good of the nation and not political reasons we could have the most perfect government in the world.

– Will Rogers; June 6, 1924.

THE SOCIALISM UNSECURITY PONZI SCHEME

The first Social Security Act was deemed unconstitutional by the Supreme Court. So to get around this a treaty was created with the United Kingdom and others. Under this treaty, you give up 15% of your pay for life to get back a small pension if you live long enough.

You can get the information from the Social Security Administration or, if they give you a problem, use the Freedom of Information Act to get out of the contract and get your money back with interest. Then you can ask for a raise because your employer does not have to pay in the Social Security for you. You may have to submit a W-8 to your employer. You can also use a W-8 to open up a bank account. Taxes can never be withheld without a Social Security numbered account. The IRS or the federal government has no authority to take any of your funds.

Object to Federal Reserve notes they are not legal tender. Lawful money is defined by Blacks Law dictionary, second edition, as "Money, which is legal tender, in payment of debts; gold and silver coined in the mint." You want to be paid in lawful money according to the Coinage Act of 1792, Article I, Section 8, Clause 5, and Article I, Section 10, Clause 1 of the Constitution of the United States.

Because the Constitution of the United States, the Supreme Law of the land, regulated monetary powers to Congress it was not within congressional authority to transfer the issuing of gold and silver coins, certificates, or unlawful Federal Reserve notes to the private Federal Reserve.

"Congress may not abdicate or transfer to others its legitimate functions."

Schechter Poultry vs. U.S. 29 U.S., 495, 55, U.S. 837.842 (1935)

Social Security is a voluntary tax. The most famous court case was Taco Bell who was sued for not hiring somebody who didn't have a Social Security number. Now on a Taco Bell application, the Social Security is optional.

Supreme Court decision IRS vs. George P. Davis

Social Security tax and income tax are both paid into the treasury and are not earmarked for any specific purpose. Because the government spent the FICA taxes and recipients' taxes, the recipients of Social Security are reliable for the payouts and administrative costs. FDR pulled the Social Security funds with other nations under the Totalization Agreement.

International Agreement – Purpose of Agreement: Sec. 233. [42 U.S.C. 433] (a) The President is authorized (subject to the succeeding provisions of this section) to enter into agreements establishing totalization arrangements between the Social Security system established by this title and the Social Security system of any foreign country, for the purposes of establishing entitlement to and the amount of old-age, survivors, disability, or derivative benefits based on a combination of an individual's periods of coverage under the Social Security system established by this title and the Social Security system of such foreign country.

Social Security is paid by the UN, IMF, and the Federal Reserve. It is a non-negotiable instrument which means a bad check is written on the check. They can't write VOID on it because the United States is a bankrupt corporation. A bankrupt cannot pay on that claim. The UN and IMF get the money from the banks who are members of the Federal Reserve. The Federal Reserve is the Fiduciary

Agent for the IMF, UN, and the World Bank. The IRS deposits goes to the Federal Reserve, not the U.S. Treasury, as in Title 26 of the International Revenue Code for debt.

The Federal Reserve started in 1913 and has never been audited. If it was ever audited, there's not telling how much money the U.S. would get.

When you get your children a Social Security number by power of attorney, you have contracted your children into slavery for benefits. A Social Security contract or a marriage license gives authority to the State to determine custody of the children. This is because you have declared that you are irresponsible. So the State makes all the decisions. The children are wards of the State and become claimants of the bankrupt government. The tax payers pay the benefits because the government doesn't have any money. A non-custodial parent may have to pay child support with no say in the upbringing lifestyle of the child. They have to pay whatever the court rules. They may not even have visitation rights. This is socialism security and you volunteered.

A child born with parents who do not have a marriage license and no Social Security number has more rights than one born with them. Because you are underage when you get your Social Security number, it should be an illegal contract.

The Founding Fathers thought that anyone giving up rights for security deserves to lose both. Why? Because give an inch, take a mile. This is what has happened. Your servant has become your master.

Did you know the average black male receives less than one year of Social Security benefits before he dies?

Can you say sucker, boys and girls? Mr. Rogers

OMB NUMBERS AND THE FEDERAL REGISTER

In the top right hand corner of IRS forms is an OMB number. For the 1040 form it is 1545-0074 which refers to Title 26 CFR 1.23-5 which is not a tax for individual income. It regards Energy Conserving Components or renewable energy resource credit. The 1040 form is used to claim certain deductions, credits or refunds, but not to satisfy a liability. The 1040 form is the legal way which a refund is claimed. This is why they withhold more money than is necessary to get you used to filing, to get a refund, not to pay taxes. The IRS regulations for Title 26 CFR 1.61-15 defines gross income as optional income. Who has optional income? The tax on individuals is Title 26 CFR 1.1-1. It has an OMB number 1545-0067 which is for the 2555 form. This is the only form required by law to satisfy their individual's liability and imposed in Section 1 Tax Imposed; The code section that imposes the income tax. This is for Foreign Earned Income. It states in bold letters: FOR USE BY US CITIZENS AND RESIDENT ALIENS ONLY.

The Federalists Papers is what the Supreme Court uses to determine what the Founding Fathers meant when they put the Constitution together. The Federalist Papers #15 states: the Unites States has an indefinite discretion to make requisitions for men and money, but they have no authority to raise either by regulations extending to the individual Citizens in America. The consequences of this is that though in theory the resolutions concerning those objections are laws constitutionally binding on the members of the Union, yet in practice they are mere recommendations which the States observe or disregard at their option. The States can disregard at their option because they created the federal government. The creation is never greater than the creator.

IRS forms are not published in the Federal Register which is the nation's legal newspaper. If there is a penalty for not filing a 1040 form there must be notice in the Federal Register. Title 44 Section 1504-1507 Example 44-1505 1…, except those not having general applicability and legal effect or effective of Federal agencies or persons in the capacity as an officers, agents or employees thereof… For the purposes of this chapter every document or order which prescribes a penalty as general applicability and legal effects. IRS regulations Title 26 601-702 in the Code of the Federal Regulation states Effect of failure to publish… thus, for example, any such matter which imposes an obligation and which is not so published or incorporated by reference adversely change or effect a persons rights. You must give notice in the Federal Register or there is no requirement to file. The IRS forms cannot be published in the Federal Reserve because they are not an agency of the federal government. In Pollack v. Farmer's Loan and Trust Company 158 US 601 (May 20, 1895) the Supreme Court ruled income tax was unconstitutional.

Title 15-17 - Commerce and Trade states: Anti-trust laws not applicable to labor organizations. The labor of a human being is not a commodity or an article of commerce. A human being is not an individual.

Occupation of Common Right such as working means that it would be legal to do it whether there was a government or not. It is a God given right. Congressional Research Service found there was no tax on Occupation of Common Right. The government can't make a right a privilege which they to do through license.

When you file a straight 1040 form (no schedule) the IRS gives you a rating of MFR01 meaning you are exempt from filing.

When talking to the IRS go on the offense, tape the conversation, be a master not a servant, prove obligation. He who asks the questions is in control. Never take anything for granted. Stand up and kick their assets all over the country.

A letter to the bank if the IRS attaches your account without due process:

I have no problem with your desire to comply with the IRS, but the U.S. Constitution is the Supreme Law of the land. You have violated my 5th Amendment right by taking my money without due process of the law. Administrative process mandate that you can only do this if your receive an assessment from the Secretary of Treasury and a court order signed by a Judge specifically stating the kind of tax that is owned and amount. The IRS must adhere to the law just as you must. Therefore, what authority are you using to take my private property money from my account? The only legal way you can take my property is by having documents mentioned above. I demand that you supply me with a copy of the documents. You can mail them or call me and I will pick them up. If you cannot produce those documents I strongly suggest that you return my private property to my account. You have five (5) business days to respond to this request. Also if you wish, you may contact the IRS to request a letter granting you and your bank immunity for my pros equity for constructive fraud and theft. I can guarantee you they will not issue that promise. You are on your own. I suggest you look at the U.S. Code Title 18 Crimes and Criminal Procedure Sec. 241. Conspiracy against rights of the citizens. I suggest you read this, as it is one of the laws you are in violation of. The IRS can not harm you if you refused to violate the laws.

U.S. Code, Title 18, Sec. 241; Crimes and Criminal Procedure

If two or more persons conspire to injure, oppress, threaten, or intimidate any person in any State, Territory, Commonwealth, Possession, or District in the free exercise or enjoyment of any right or privilege secured to him by the Constitution or laws of the United States, or because of his having so exercised the same; or If two or more persons go in disguise on the highway, or on the premises of another, with intent to prevent or hinder his free exercise or enjoyment of any right or privilege so secured - They shall be fined under this title or imprisoned not more than ten years, or both; and if death results from the acts committed in violation of this section or if such acts include kidnapping or an attempt to kidnap, aggravated sexual abuse or an attempt to commit aggravated sexual abuse, or an attempt to kill, they shall be fined under this title or imprisoned for any term of years or for life, or both, or may be sentenced to death.

"I have never objected to paying taxes but I do object to government eating up the real wealth of this country on the pretext of giving it back to the people. It never gets back to the people." Henry Ford

DE-CODING THE INTERNAL ROBBING SERVICE

Lenin said "Confuse the meaning of words and you confuse the mind." A Citizen of the 50 states is not under IRS Code as a United States citizen, a United States resident, or an individual but as an alien. Any of the 50 states is a foreign country, is "without" the United States, is a foreign government and are not states within the United States.

"Congress may provide its own definition for the terms used. The student should be aware of number of general definition contained in the 26 IRC..." Malat v. Riddell.

In statue ad the word *only* after the words *include, includes,* and *including.* "It is a well established principle of law that all federal legislation applies only within the territorial jurisdiction of the United States unless a contrary intent appears." Foley Brothers., Inc. v. Filardo, 336, U.S. 281 (1948)

"The District of Columbia is not a "state" within the meaning of the Constitution." – U.S. v. Virginia, 1805

1939 Code: [Sections 3797 (a) (10)](When Alaska and Hawaii were both Territories) "State – The term "State" shall be construed to include [only] the Territories and the District of Columbia, where such construction is necessary to carry out provisions of this title." (Note: Because the District of Columbia was never one of the 50 states of the Union, it is obvious that the IRS Word of Art for "State" does not mean the "50 states").

1954 Code: (When Alaska became one of the 49 states and Hawaii is the only Territory) "Amended 1954 Sec. 7701(a) 10 by striking out "Territories," and substituting "Territory of Hawaii." "State [26 USC 7701(a) (10)] "The term State shall be construed to include [only] the Territory of Hawaii and the District of Columbia..."

The IRS code capitalized State when referring to the territorial States and District of Columbia and uses the lowercase state when referring to the 50 sovereign states.

On August 21, 1959 when Hawaii became a state. The definition of "State" became "The term State shall be construed to include [only] the District of Columbia..." (Note the exclusion of the Territory of Hawaii which has now moved into the classification of the "50 states").

3121(e) of the Internal Revenue Code [related to "employee" taxed] defines State as follows: "For the purposes of this chapter – (1) STATE – The term "State" includes [only] the District of Columbia, the Commonwealth of Puerto Rico, the Virgin Islands, Guam and America Samoa."

26 CFR 1.911-2(g) "The term "United States" when used in a geographical sense includes any territory under the sovereignty of the United States. It includes the States, the District of Columbia, the possessions and territories of the United States, the territorial waters of the United States, the air space over the United States, and the seabed and subsoil of those submarine areas which are adjacent to the territorial waters of the United States and over which the United States has exclusive rights, in accordance with international law..."

When you don't add *only* after *includes* and *including* as in Section 7701 (29) (C) "The terms "includes" and "including" when used in a definition contained in this title shall not be deemed to exclude other things otherwise within the meaning of the term defined."

Treasury Definition 3980, Vol. 29, January-December, 1927, pgs. 64 and 65 defines the words includes and including as "(1) To comprise, comprehend, or embrace… (2) To enclose within; contain; confine… But granting that the word "including" is a term of enlargement, it is clear that it only performs that office by introducing the specific elements constituting the enlargement. It thus, and thus only, enlarges the otherwise more limited, preceding general language… The words "including" is obviously used in the sense of its synonyms, comprising; comprehending; embracing."

When the IR Code term "United States" does mean the 50 states it must specifically say so, as in the following:

- Miscellaneous Excise Taxes Section 4612 (a) Definitions. – For the purposes of this subchapter… (4) "United States" (A) In general. – The term "United States" means the 50 States, the District of Columbia, the Commonwealth of Puerto Rico, a possession of the United States…"
- Section 6103(b)(5)(a) 00 For the purposes of this section… "The term "state" means and of the 50 States, the District of Columbia, the Commonwealth of Puerto Rico, the [U.S.] Virgin Islands the Canal Zone, Guam, American Samoa…"

A quote from the Revenue law of 1913: "The Act expressly directs: That the word

"State" or "United States" when used in this Section shall be construed to include any Territory, Alaska, the District of Columbia, Puerto Rico, and the Philippine Islands when such construction is necessary to carry out its provisions." The authors continue, "The tax is, therefore, levied only in Alaska, the District of Columbia, Puerto Rico, and the Philippine Islands. If the tax were to be levied within the states of the Union, it would have been required to specifically states such."

26 CFR §31. 3401 (c) Employee. – "For purposes of this chapter, the term employee includes an officer, employee or elected official of the United States [Government], a [federal] State, Territory, Puerto Rico or any political subdivision thereof, or the District of Columbia, or any agency or instrumentality of any one or more of the foregoing. The term employee also includes an officer of a corporation."

Federal Register, Tuesday, September 7, 1943, Section 404.104, pg12267: Employee: "The term employee specifically includes officers and employees whether elected or appointed, of the United States, a state, territory, or political subdivision thereof or the District of Columbia or any agency or instrumentality of any one or more of the foregoing."

26 IRC §3401 (a) Wages. – For the purposes of this chapter [Chapter 24, Collection of Income Tax at Source on Wages], the term "wages" means all remuneration (other than fees paid to a public official) for services performed by an employee [of the government]…"

Congress taxes income not compensation, such as wages and salaries. Pay from a job is a wage, which is not taxable. – Conner v. U.S. 303 F. Supp. 1187 (1969)

26 CFR §1.1-1 (c) "Who is a citizen. Every person born or naturalized in the United States and subject to its jurisdiction is a citizen."

Citizen of U.S. (3 AM Jur2d Aliens Section 116) "A person born or Naturalized in the United States and Subject to its jurisdiction.

Individual. – [5 USC §552 (a) (2)] "The term Individual means a citizen of the [District] United States or an alien lawfully admitted for permanent residence."

§7343 Person. – "Person, as used in this chapter, includes and officer or employee of a corporation or member or employee of a partnership, who as such officer, employee or member is under a duty to perform the act in which the violation occurs" [Does not include the natural person, or Citizen].

§7701 (a) (14) Taxpayer. – The term "taxpayer" means any person subject to any internal revenue tax.

§7701 (a) (26) Trade of Business. – Includes the performance of the functions of a public [government] office.

Within the United States. – Within the boundaries of territories belonging to the United States. Without the United States. – In one of the 50 states or in an inter-nation country. (Foreign)

The 16th Amendment which allegedly authorizes the income tax has never been ratified by the necessary number of states.

"I want to be sure he is a ruthless son of a bitch, that he will do what he's told, that every income tax return I want to see I see, that he will go after our enemies and not our friends. Now it's as simple as that. If he isn't, he doesn't get the job. Richard Nixon Tapes from May of 1971, describing his criteria for a new IRS commissioner. "Perspectives", Newsweek. January 13, 1997, p. 23.

"The right to labor and to its protection from unlawful interference is a constitutional as well as a common-law right. Every man has a natural right to the fruits of his own industry." 48 American Jurisprudent 2d, Labor and Labor Relations § 2

"Every man has a natural right to the fruits of his own labor, as generally admitted; and no other person can rightfully deprive him of those fruits, and appropriate them against his will". The Antelope, 23 US 66,120

"The property which every man has is his own labor, as it is the original foundation of all other property, so it is the most sacred and inviolable. The patrimony of the poor man lies in the strength and dexterity of his own hands, and to hinder his employing this strength and dexterity in what manner he thinks proper, without injury to his neighbor, is a plain violation of this most sacred property." Butchers' Union Co. v. Crescent City, 111 US 746 (May 5, 1884).

"…liberty denotes, not merely freedom from bodily restraint, but also the right of the individual to contract, to engage in any of the common occupations of life, to acquire useful knowledge, to marry, establish a home, and bring up children, to worship God according to the dictates of his own conscience…The established doctrine is that this liberty may not be interfered with, under the guise of protecting public interest, by legislative action…" Meyer v. State of Nebraska, 262 U.S. 390; 43 S.Ct. 625 (June 4, 1923).

THE UNFEDERAL RESERVE

The Federal Reserve Act of 1913 was 35% American owned by Rockefeller and J. P. Morgan interests and 65% foreigner owned by the Rothschild's, Lazerd Fresres (Eugine Mayor), Israel Moses Sieff, Kuhn Loeb Company, Paul Warburg Company, Lehman Brothers, and Goldman Sachs.

On November 22, 1910, Senator Nelson Aldrich, maternal grandfather of Nelson Aldrich Rockefeller, and the Monetary Commission at the J. P. Morgan hunting club on Jekyll Island, Georgia drafted the unpopular Owen-Glass Bill. Later it was changed deceptively to the Federal Reserve Act. It was passed on December 23, 1913 while the majority of opposing Congressmen were on Christmas vacation. Banker President Woodrow Wilson, who later on his death bed said he sold out his country, immediately signed it.

How it works:
1. The U.S. Bureau of Printing and Engraving prints the Federal Reserve notes.
2. The Federal Reserve pays 5 cents per bill regardless of denomination for printing costs.
3. The United States orders the U.S. Bureau of Printing and Engraving to print U.S. Treasury Bonds.
4. The Federal Reserve purchases the U.S. Treasury Bonds redeemable at full price plus interest with the Federal Reserve note they purchased for 5 cents.
5. If the United States needs credit, instead of cash, it is done the same way, except the Federal Reserve saves the printing costs.

The Federal Reserve gets money for nothing. The Collateral the government uses is the Peoples' production, property and land. That is all land without allodial land patents. To legally own anything you must buy it with lawful money. If you buy something with more than $20 in gold or silver it is protected under the 7th Amendment of the Bill of Rights. If you buy it with unlawful money you have custody but you don't legally own it.

Thomas Jefferson said, "If our nation can issue a dollar bond, it can issue a dollar bill. The element that makes the bond good also makes the bill good. The difference between the bond and the bill is that the bond lets money brokers collect twice the amount of the bond plus interest. Whereas the bill pays nobody but those who contribute directly in some way. The People are basis for government credit! Why then cannot the People have the benefit of their own credit by receiving non-interest leaving currency, instead of bankers receiving the benefit of the Peoples' credit in interest bearing bonds? It is absurd to say that our country can issue $30 million in bonds and not $30 million in currency! Both are promises to pay: But one promise fattens the usurers and the other helps the people."

Benjamin Franklin was in England in 1763 was asked why the colonies were so prosperous while England was having hard times. He replied, "That's simple. It's only because in the colonies we issue our own money called colonial script." With this information, the Bank of England forced Parliament to pass a bill to stop the colonies from issuing their own money. Franklin said, "Within one year from the date Parliament passed this bill, the streets of the colonies were filled with unemployed

Americans." Later, Franklin said, "The colonies would gladly have come to the little tax on tea and other matters, had it not been that England took away from the colonies their money, which created unemployment and dissatisfaction." The War of Independence was caused by the Bank of England taking away the citizens unborrowed money.

During the War, the unborrowed currency issued was called Continentals. The English counterfeited the Continentals causing an abundance of money in circulation causing inflation.

In 1802, Thomas Jefferson said… "I believe the banking institutions are more dangerous to our liberties than standing armies. If the American people ever allow private banks to control the issue of their currency, first buy inflation, then buy deflation, the banks and the corporations that will grow around the banks will deprive the people of all property. Until their children wake up homeless on the continent, their Fathers' conquered."

When the War Between the States broke out, the European bankers tried to charge up to 36% interest on loans. Lincoln said, "The money borrows prey among the nation and times of peace and conspire against it in times of adversity. It is more despotic than a monarchy, more insolent autocracy, more selfish than bureaucracy. It denounces, as public enemies, all who question its methods or through light upon its enemies. I have two great enemies, the Southern Army in front of me and the bankers in the rear. Of the two, the one in my rear is my greatest foe."

To combat the banker debt-free and interest free United States Notes called "Greenbacks" were issued. Lincoln said, "We have given the people of the Republic the greatest blessing they had ever had, their own currency to pay their own debts."

Bankers fought back with money influencing the lawyer Congress to add "exception clauses" to the Law requiring duties or imports and interest on the public debt owed to the bankers to be paid only in gold. The Bankers added a 185% surcharge on the price of gold purchased with Greenbacks which meant it took $285 in Greenbacks for $100 in gold. The 185% was added to the cost of the goods increasing prices causing people to falsely believe the Greenbacks were inflationary.

An editorial in Rothschild's London Times said of Greenbacks, "If this mischief financial policy, which has its origin in the American Republic, shall become permanent, then that government will furnish its own money without cost. It will pay off its debts and be without debt; it will have all the money necessary to carry on its commerce. It will become prosperous without precedent in the history of the world. The brains and wealth of all countries will go to America. That government must be destroyed or it will destroy every monarchy on the globe."

On June 4, 1963, President John. F. Kennedy authorized $4 billion to be issued in the United States silver certificates. Kennedy stated on November 12, 1963, in a speech at Colombia University, 10 days before his assassination, "The high office of President has been used to foment a plot to destroy the American's freedom, and before I leave office I must inform the citizen of his plight."

Immediately after being sworn in, President Lyndon B. Johnson went to the front of the plane and made a call to stop the Silver Certificates and destroy those that had been printed. Johnson said, in 1964 (the year before all silver coins were no longer minted), "Silver had become too valuable to be used as money."

Johnson said, in a speech in 1964, "Some have asked whether silver coins will disappear, the answer is definitely--- no! Our present coins won't disappear and they won't even become rarities… If anybody has the idea of holding silver coins, let me say this, the Treasury has a lot of silver on hand and it can be, and it will be used to keep the price of silver in line with its value and our present silver coin. There will be no profit in holding them out of circulation for the value of their silver content.

On July 23, 1965, under orders from the Federal Reserve, Johnson signed a bill replacing silver coins with cooper clad coins and abolished silver certificates.

TITLE 12, CHAPTER 3, SUBCHAPTER XII, Sec. 411. Issuance to Reserve Banks; nature of obligation; redemption. Federal Reserve notes, to be issued at the discretion of the Board of Governors of the Federal Reserve System for the purpose of making advances to Federal Reserve banks through the Federal Reserve agents as hereinafter set forth and for no other purpose, are authorized. The said notes shall be obligations of the United States and shall be receivable by all national and member banks and Federal Reserve banks and for all taxes, customs, and other public dues. They shall be redeemed in lawful money on demand at the Treasury Department of the United States, in the city of Washington, District of Columbia, or at any Federal Reserve Bank.

FYI - Congress repudiated their promise to redeem their IOUs, in 1933, in House Joint Resolution 192. Obviously, the federal government must accept their notes as tender. But they are 'legal tender' to the private sector due to universal 'voluntary' enrollment into FICA / Social Security. All "contributors" are equally liable thus cannot object to the tender of "their" notes.

"Federal reserve notes are legal tender in absence of objection thereto." MacLeod v. Hoover (1925) 159 La 244, 105 So. 305

After 1935, enumerated Socialists could no longer object.

Money not backed by gold or silver, it is unlawful money. As a matter of fact, because of the deficit, every American owes over forty thousand dollars in counterfeit money.

The Bill of Rights, Article VII. – In Suits at common law, where the value in controversy shall exceed twenty dollars, the right of trial by jury shall be preserved, and no fact tried by a jury, shall be otherwise re-examined in any Court of the United States, than according to the rules of the common law.

In other words, in order for anything you own to be protected by the Constitution, you must buy it with lawful money, which is gold or silver, of more than twenty dollars. Federal Reserve notes are promissory notes, not backed by gold or silver. Therefore, anything you buy with Federal Reserve notes is not really yours and can be taken away.

First National Bank of Montgomery vs. Jerome Daly – Federal Reserve Notes are void

First National Bank of Montgomery vs. Jerome Daly, Dec. 9, 1968 (Justice Court, Credit River Township, Scott County, Minnesota), also known as the Credit River Case, was a case tried before a Justice of the Peace in Minnesota in 1968. The decision in that case, although it was ultimately reversed, is sometimes cited by opponents of the United States banking system.

The trial
-- An attorney named Jerome Daly was a defendant in a civil case in Credit River Township, Scott County, Minnesota, heard on December 9, 1968. The plaintiff was the First National Bank of Montgomery, which had foreclosed on Daly's property for nonpayment of the mortgage, and was seeking to evict him from the property.
-- Daly based his defense on the argument that the bank had not actually loaned him any money but had simply created credit on its books. Daly argued that the bank had thus not given him anything of value and was not entitled to the property that secured the loan. The jury and the justice of the peace, Martin V. Mahoney, agreed with this argument. The jury returned a verdict for the defendant, and the Justice of the Peace declared that the mortgage was "null and void" and that the bank was not entitled to possession of the property. The Justice admitted in his order that his decision might run counter to provisions in the Minnesota Constitution and some Minnesota statutes, but contended that such provisions were "repugnant" to the Constitution of the United States and the Bill of Rights in the Minnesota Constitution.

The result

The immediate effect of the decision was that Daly did not have to repay the mortgage or relinquish the property. The case and its reasoning have subsequently been cited as nullifying the U.S. banking system and in particular the practice of fractional-reserve banking.

However, the bank appealed the next day, and the decision was ultimately nullified on the grounds that a Justice of the Peace did not have the power to make such a ruling. The nullification did not address the case's merits.

Because the decision was nullified, the case has no value as precedent. However, it is still cited by groups who support a government owned central bank or oppose the Federal Reserve System; such groups argue the case demonstrates that the Federal Reserve System is unconstitutional. A U.S. District Court decision in Utah in 2008 mentioned half a dozen such citations, noting that similar arguments have "repeatedly been dismissed by the courts as baseless" and that "courts around the country have repeatedly dismissed efforts to void loans based on similar assertions."

Jerome Daly's other attacks on the banking system

The defendant, Jerome Daly, was a longtime tax protester. He was convicted of willfully failing to file federal income tax returns for the years 1967 and 1968. In rejecting his appeal, the United States Court of Appeals for the Eighth Circuit noted: "Defendant's fourth contention involves his seemingly incessant attack against the federal reserve and monetary system of the United States. His apparent thesis is that the only 'Legal Tender Dollars' are those which contain a mixture of gold and silver and that only those dollars may be constitutionally taxed. This contention is clearly frivolous. Daly had been an attorney, but was later disbarred by a decision of the Minnesota Supreme Court.

Martin v. Mahoney Justice of the Peace Credit River Township Scott County, Minnesota – Federal Reserve Notes declared unconstitutional null and void by the court.

Note: The Defendant, (Attorney) Jerome Daley, shortly after the above Court declared the above decision, again brought the issue of the Federal Reserve Notes before the Courts. On Appeal to a Federal Court; the Federal Judicial Officers publicly ridiculed Mr. Daley for challenging the validity of the Notes of the Federal Reserve Bank and had Mr. Daley *"disbarred"*; from practicing law (United States v. Jerome Daly, 481 F.2d. 28). This "act" of our Federal Judicial Officers to *"disbar"* a fellow member of the *"Bar"* for questioning the validity of the monetary system of the United States raises the question as to who the Federal Judicial Officers are employed by? It is obvious that they are employed by the International Banking Cartels; NOT THE PEOPLE OF THE UNITED STATES.

"Give me control of a nation's money and I care not who makes the laws." Rothschild

ID CARDS

In America, we are taxed, licensed, regulated, monitored, attacked, robbed, jailed, and spied on more than any other time in our history. The worst part is that it is all being done to us by the very government established for our protection. The fact that nearly all of our rights, privileges, and immunities have been gradually taken away is now self-evident.

Freedom and liberty are nothing more than illusions. The once proud United States of America has greatly "Altered its State," and that a more appropriate name for it would be "The United Slaves of Amerika." Any American who has gone to great lengths to divorce himself and his assets from the clutches of the government, may discover that no matter how resourceful and inventive he has been with his offshore pursuits, his identity, as recorded by his country of birth and/or citizenship, remains his Achilles heel until he successfully disassociates himself from his identity as a fictional entity.

The identification of individuals has been with us for centuries. You identity may represent your position of honor, status, or standing among other men and women. You can be self-identified, or identified by others. If you are self-identified, it is usually accomplished by reputation, occupation, noble deeds, character, etc.

Being self-identified carries a natural place of honor or dishonor among peers. You are either honest, trustworthy, and of good moral character, or you are not. The reputation, honor and identification of a good and lawful man or woman, precedes them. They are known for who they are and who they stand for. This form of identification, at its best, is accomplished by a lot of hard work, and adhering to the highest standards of ethics and moral character.

The majority of the people in the world carry identification cards granted or issued by others. This allows others to create the persona and the lawful standing of the man or woman. It is an established fact that the created can never be greater than the creator. Whatever the creator creates, he controls. Also, the creator cannot elevate the created above the standing of the creator. For example, a city mayor cannot appoint a state governor. Although, most people carry ID cards, they have absolutely no foundation in law, whatsoever. There is not law written that makes it mandatory for one to carry any type of ID. The only time anyone is required to have ID is to excess so called privileges and benefits granted by the issuing party. If you have no need for special privileges and benefits granted by others, there is no need for an ID card. Keep in mind that the government has nothing to give. It produces nothing. In order to bestow a special privilege or benefit on one person, the government must take from another. All those who receive privileges, benefits, and handouts from government, that is money not earned, are doing nothing more than robbing their neighbors by plunder. No matter what type of ID you carry, one thing is for sure, you did not issue it to yourself. You willfully applied for the ID hoping to receive some type of special privilege or benefit granted by the authority.

For clarity, it is necessary to define the difference between natural Rights, which are unalienable and not within the power of government to grant and privileges and benefits, which clearly are. Natural Rights include but not limited to the right: contract, work, get married, use public roads, own property, open a business, choose your own destiny, worship, defend yourself, etc. Privileges and benefits may include any activity that gives the beneficiary a special advantage not usually granted to the general public. These special advantages are usually granted by way of a license or permit. A license is defined as "permission given by a competent authority to do something that would otherwise be unlawful." The question is, do you, as most people believe, needed permission as in a license or permit to contract, work, get married, use the public roads, own property, open a business, choose your own destiny, worship, defend themselves, etc.? The answer is you don't. That is unless you voluntarily, by your own free will and violation, apply for, or granted, and accept the fictitious privilege or benefit being offered. Thereby placing yourself in a state of "voluntary servitude."

By way or endorsing this fact, the Constitution of the United States of America clearly states that the condition of "involuntary" servitude shall forever be prohibited. The keyword here is involuntary. This means that your natural Rights cannot be converted to privileges without your consent and privileges cannot be converted to rights without consent of the authority.

Although there are many types of identification the most common are the drivers license, passports, social security card, birth certificate, employee ID, student cards, credit cards, military discharge/separation, selective service registration, union memberships, professional licenses, married certificates, and baptismal. There are many more. Several peculiar things happen when you voluntarily apply for and accept identifying documents for government or government created entities. They are:

1. Name change: your persona changes to a legal fiction with no persona as a man or woman standing in judicio court whatsoever. This accomplished by changing your lawfully given name to that of a legal fiction. That legal fiction is represented by your name spelled in all capital letters, and may include initials. All government and corporate entities currently issuing ID cards today are legal fictions. They only exist on paper. They do not die like a man or woman. They live on perpetuity. Therefore, when you are identified by a legal fiction, you must become a legal fiction as well. Remember the created can never be greater than the creator.

2. Creates a nexus: A "nexus" is defined as a connection; tie; link. A connected series or group; a joining, fastening; to bind. That is, a firm legal attachment has been made between you and the issuing party. By carrying a state issued ID card you are placed "within" the issuing state as a resident of the state. Res = thing, Ident = identified. A thing identified is no longer a man or woman.

3. Forms an adhesion contract or agreement: The distinctive feature of an adhesion contract or agreement is that the weaker party has no realistic choice as to the terms. An exampled of an adhesion contract is when you voluntarily apply for and receive a driver license. Once the driver license has been issued, the licensee is legally bound by the vehicle code. You, the applicant have voluntarily converted your right to use the public roads as a motorist into a privileged activity as a driver.

All power rests with "We the People" after all it is "We the People" who created the government in the first place. Since the created cannot be greater than the creator, it must follow that the government is something less than the creator and must by its own nature be the creator's servant. This is true until your voluntarily allow the servant to be your master which is what most people have done to themselves by making public servants their masters. The government cannot do anything for you or against you without your consent. Your consent is either given in writing, by our verbal consent or by your silence. A maxim of law says: "the law does not require impossibilities." Another maxim is: "where the Laws of Holy Scriptures and the laws of man are at variance, the former shall always be obeyed." A maxim of law is something that has been ruled on so many times that it is a firmly established truth, and is no longer up for debate. In order to get any government privilege or benefit, you must fill out a form and provide false or hearsay information.

Here is an example: John was stopped by the Highway Patrol for not having a license plate on his car. After the stop it was discovered that he did not have a driver's license as well. Attempts to interrogate him proved fruitless to the officer. John remained silent except to answer the officer's questions with his own questions. Frustrated, the officer arrested John and brought him before the local magistrate Judge to answer for his terrible crimes.

Before being forced to come before the Judge, John managed to get some paperwork from his car. The paperwork consisted of more than one hundred court cites from the Supreme Court on driving clearly stating that a driver's license was only required for commercial activity. That is, the transportation of "person" and property "for hire" like a taxi driver, chauffeur, coachman, etc.

The Judge looked at John's paperwork, nodded in agreement, and said, "Yes, I understand this." The Judge then wadded up all of John's papers into a ball and threw them across the courtroom like a spoiled child. He then pointed his finger at John and said, "I don't care what that says, I say, you must have a driver's license and registration! John said, "Judge, I don't want to offend you or this court. So, exactly what is it that this court wants me to do in order to clear up this matter?" "Young man, I want you to get a driver's license and registration," said the Judge. "Fine," said John, "let me understand this: applying for a driver's license and registration will clear up this matter?" The Judge said, "Yes it will." "Okay, Judge," said John, "I'll do what this court orders, provided that I don't have to lie in order to get the license and registration. Scriptures say that I cannot bear false witness." "I never asked you to lie," said the Judge. "You have ten days from today to do what this court has ordered you to do."

John went to the Department of Motor Vehicles and proceeded to fill out the required forms. He crossed out "First name", "M.I.", and "Last name" from the form, and wrote, "Given name" and "Surname". Then he wrote his name in proper upper and lower case English letters. What's your address? asked the form. "General delivery", wrote John. Social Security number? None. Date of birth? Unknown. Are you a Florida resident? No. Are you a U.S. citizen? No.

The reasons are:

1. Men and women do not have first, middle, and last names. They have given names and surnames. Anyone claiming to have a first, middle, and last name is a legal fiction.

2. You cannot claim to have a street address that belongs to you. The reason being is that when you move you cannot take the address with you. Therefore, the address must belong to someone else. The only address that you own is "general delivery" which is a traditionally vested Right. You can receive "general delivery" wherever you go. The only condition is that you must go to the post office to pick up your "posts."

3. Even if you think that you have a Social Security number, think again. The name on the card is not yours because it is all capital letters, and the number is not yours because you did not create it. You can honestly say before any court that you have never been issued a Social Security number in your name.

4. Were you conscience when you were born? How do you know from first hand knowledge, the date on which you were born? Did you mother tell you this date? Did she ever lie to you? What about the Easter Bunny and Santa Claus? How about an alleged Birth Certificate? Were you there when this document was created? Did you sign it? The fact is that your date of birth is nothing but hearsay. Everything is hearsay as it applies to you unless you have firsthand knowledge of it.

5. Resident of the State means. Res = thing, Ident = identified, which together equals a thing identified, and is no longer a man or woman. Does the term resident apply to you?

6. The United States is defined as District of Columbia, Puerto Rico, Virgin Islands, American Sonoma, and Northern Marinas Islands. The United States is a corporation and is not the same as the United States of America. As in, the fifty states. Claiming to be a US citizen voluntarily makes you a corporate political citizen subject and person under the 14th Amendment to the Constitution of the United States of America.

John completed the application and gave it to a clerk, who promptly told John that his application had been denied. John called the supervisor over and explains his situation. "I have to get a driver license and registration," says John. "It's a court order." "We'd like to comply, but you are simply not eligible," the supervisor replied. "You are not a resident and you do not have a Social Security number. We cannot issue you a license." "I don't think the Judge will believe that I tried to get a license," said John. "Will you write a short note to explain why I was denied?" The supervisor agreed and wrote a not explaining the reason why John was denied. John returned to the court with a note form the DMV and his rejected application form. "Judge," he said, "I tried my very best to comply with this courts order to get a driver license and registration, and here are the results of my efforts." The Judge reviewed the paperwork and said, "Fine, that's all I ever asked you to do. Now get out of my courtroom!"

Scriptures teach us that if your adversaries want to walk one mile, walk two, and if they want your cloak, give them your tunic as well. Remember, the Law does not require impossibilities. You will find that no matter what your public servants order you to do, tell the truth, and you will simply be ineligible. The Law can only mandate performance on artificial entities. If their laws applied to you then they must make a provision to make you eligible without making a lie, or forcing you into a condition of peonage and involuntary servitude which is prohibited in all the fifty states. Allowing others to identify you can be deadly when claiming your natural Rights. If you feel that you must carry some form of identification, then create it yourself or have it made to your specifications. Only God is above the authority of natural man. Holy Scriptures make it very clear that you cannot serve God and have other masters.

The road to personal freedom can be accomplished in three easy steps:

1. Know and understand exactly who you are. Are you a legal fiction in a franchise to be pillage and plunder, or a man or woman? If you are a man or woman then you must allow the fictional persona which is your name in all capital letters to die and then bury it. Never answer to or recognize this name again. Any property that you may have recorded or registered with your fictional name is subject to attack. Take all steps necessary to transfer your property out of the fictional name. An Unincorporated Business Trust is a viable option. Note that all statues and codes called color law are applicable to residents and persons only. That is artificial entities. Public Law which is real law is routed in the Holy Scriptures and applies to men and women. According to statue and code, a person is defined as a corporation, franchise, an individual, and sometimes a human being, which are all artificial entities.

Balentine Law Dictionary (1930):
  * human being. See monster.
  * monster. A human being by birth, but in some part resembling a lower animal. "A monster, hath no inheritable blood, and cannot be heir to any land."

The Holy Scriptures tell us that in the beginning God created man in His image. He did not create corporations, franchises, individuals, human beings or monsters. These are the creations of Satan, created in Satan's image.

2. Know what your law is. One is either under God's Laws which stand as eternal truth can never change, or, one is under the thousands of arbitrary and conflicting man made laws that can and will change on a political whim. Man's laws are in direct conflict with God's laws. It is a maxim of Law that where the laws of the Holy Scriptures and the laws of man are at variance, the former shall always be obeyed. The choice is totally yours. The government cannot force you to violate Scriptural Law. That's a fact.

3. Know to whom you belong and serve. Either you belong to and serve God or you belong to and serve the state. You cannot serve two masters. Liberty and freedom are won on a personal level.

Someone else can't do it for you; you must take steps to gain your own freedom through personal education and action. A famous quote says, "The surest way for evil to prevail is for good men to do nothing." In doing nothing, you will have no cause to complain when evil prevails.

You must fully understand the dangers of accepting and using the fictional name which is your name in all capital letters given as a slave name. To drive the point home so that you'll never forget it, the following questions and answer and explanations are given:

Have you ever asked yourself why it is, that you are never allowed to enter a courtroom as a plaintiff or defendant in Propria Persona? Propia Persona commonly known as Pro Per simply means that you are entering the court as the person in the subject matter, in the flesh, as a man or woman. The court may reluctantly allow you to enter the court Pro Se which is representing the person in the subject matter or the court will allow an attorney to represent the person in the subject of matter. But, never, Pro Per.

The reason is because you, the man or woman, are not the person in the subject matter. How can a fiction appear in the flesh? The cause of action is always against the fiction. This is evident by the way your name is spelled within the courts document with all capital letters. All courts in the US are legal fictions which are military courts against civilians under the Emergency War Powers Act of March 9, 1933. The courts of today are no longer under Judicial Branch of government; they are under the Executive Branch of government. This is evident by the gold fringed flag in every courtroom. A gold fringed flag is a military flag (Title 4, USC 1). The flag serves as notice to all that they are entering a military court. The courts can only prosecute another illegal fiction, except in cases of Common Law, crimes such as rape, murder, robbery, and other trespasses.

The trick that the court uses to get you to voluntarily subject yourself to their jurisdiction is by sending out or serving defective service, defective warrants, notices to appear, or similar official sounding papers. Defective service, simply means that due process of the Law is not being followed. They are, in actuality, all invitations.

Defective service which is usually associated with victimless crimes becomes perfected when one answers to the defective service, by voluntarily walking into their courtroom, standing behind the Bar, and entering into the benefits of discussion with the court. Simply by answering when your name is called is all that it takes. Military courts do not recognize positive Law. Attempting to introduce the Constitution for Holy Scriptures into one of these Admiralty courts, will swiftly result in being found in contempt of court. This may be followed by jail time and/or fines. Due process is guaranteed under the Constitution for the United States of America. In order for due process of Law to take place, the court must do the following:

1. The person in the subject matter must be properly named. If you are a man or woman and not a legal fiction, this means your name cannot, under any circumstances, be spelt in all capital letters of contain initials.

2. The court must issue a summons for your appearance. That summons must be under official court seal and personally signed by the presiding Judge not a court clerk or with no signature which is common.

3. To that summons, must be attached, a sworn complain of a damaged victim or injured party. Without an injured party there could be no crime. The State cannot claim to be an injured party. The State is a fiction and cannot be damaged. Also, the State has a vested interest in finding you guilty in whatever violation they can dream up to raise revenue, and therefore is a bias witness against you. The court, State, and the police, all share in the fine taxes so called bail, etc.

4. The summons must then be given to the county Sheriff; then the Sheriff must personally handle and serve the summons upon you.

5. When all of the above is accomplished you must appear or a warrant will be issued for your arrest.

You may ask yourself why it is, that in order to legally change your name it has to be done through the court system. It is because the name you are trying to change does not belong to you. It is the name that the system created for you. After all is said and done, you will have accomplished nothing more than getting another slave name written in all capital letters. A man's name written in all capital letters is known in closed circles as a 'nom de guerre,' or war name as translated from their French origin.

In the movie Roots by Alex Haley, there was a King from Africa named Kunta Kinte. He was taken captive and brought to America as a slave. His slave master didn't like Kinta Kinte having the name of a King, and was promptly given the name of Toby by his new master. This is essentially what has happened to nearly everyone in America. The only difference is that Kunta Kinte did not have a choice. If you have accepted your slave name and carry their ID to confirm it, then it was done so, voluntary. The fact is, you have the power to change your lawfully given name at anytime you wish.

Remember, if it looks like a duck, walks like a duck, and acts like a duck, it surely must be a duck. If you, walk, and act as a slave, the system will treat you as a slave.

ROAD BLOCKS AND SEARCHES

Road blocks and searches are in violation of the U.S. Constitution, which police officers are sworn to uphold. Here are some questions to ask them:

Did you receive any instruction articles from your training school, which included a copy of the U.S. Constitution and the State Constitution where you reside? Were you requested to purchase one and study it?

Did your training instructor recommend that you study the Constitutions?

Did your training instructor give you a test on your knowledge of the U.S. Constitution and State Constitution where you reside? Have you ever wondered why you were asked to sign and swear and oath before God that you would uphold the U.S. Constitution and Constitution of the State where you reside and work, but were never requested to read or study the Constitutions?

Did you know that when you issue a traffic ticket, you are issuing an illegal warrant and that only a Judge can issue a warrant?

Does it not seem odd that you were given a test on certain aspects on your training and never requested to swear before God that you had learned such instructions and/or qualified for certain certifications thereof, but instead you were requested and mandated that you swear before God to uphold a document that you have probably never read, never studied, and was never required to study?

Did you know that your state laws do not overrule the U.S. Constitution and that your State Supreme Court cases do not overrule the U.S. Constitution or overrule any of the U.S. circuit court cases?

Did you know that one of the most celebrated U.S. Supreme Court cases in all of our American history states, "All laws which are repugnant to the Constitution are null and void"? Marbury v. Madison, 5 U.S. (1 Cranch) 137, 2L Ed. 60 (February 1803) An unconstitutional act is not law, it confers no rights, it imposes no duties, affords no protection, creates no office, it is legal contemplation, as inoperative as though it had never passed. Norton v. Shelby County, 118 U.S. 425 (1886)

Did you know that your city and county ordinances were mostly unconstitutional? Most attorneys will not go against the hands that feed them so generously. They take your case for show to relieve you of your money. When you go to court, the Judge is your enemy and your lawyer is an enemy spy. The lawyers' first duty is to the court, not you.

Did you know the U.S. Constitution is the Supreme Law of the land and all courts are duty bound on oath to support and defend the U.S. Constitution as well as the State Constitution, where they reside, which must be in full agreement with the U.S. Constitution? "Were rights secured by the Constitution were involved, there can be no rule making or legislation which would abrogate them. Miranda v. Arizona, 384 U.S. 436, 86 S. Ct. 1602 (1996)

Article VI Sec. 2 "This Constitution, and the Laws of the United States, which shall be made in Pursuance thereof; and all Treaties made, or which shall be made, under the Authority of the United States, shall be the supreme Law of the Land; and the Judges in every State shall be bound thereby; any Thing in the Constitution or Laws of any State to the Contrary notwithstanding."

Does it not seem odd that you, as a police officer, are presumed to know the law of the land, the U.S. Constitution, when you are doing your duty every day, but yet your training instructor never gave you a test or evaluated your knowledge thereof?

Does it not seem odd that you were not given more hours of instruction regarding the U.S. Constitution, especially when it was mandated that you swear before God that you would uphold this document before the state would verify you as a police officer?

Did you know the U.S. Constitution it is your proper and correct basis of all your duties that you perform each and every day? Why would your training instructors and superiors never request that you study them? Could it be that your superiors do not want you asking too many questions regarding your duties, for fear you might become knowledgeable to their game, then the revenue that you've been bringing in will diminish? Could it be if they lose you to protect them and bring in the money, their jobs would be in jeopardy?

When you are making an arrest of a person, doesn't it seem logical for you to use the correct method and procedure, so that you will not violate that persons secured and God given Rights?

Are you familiar with the Declaration of Independence, the document that our U.S. Constitution was drafted from and is in fact the enabling clause, which gives our U.S. Constitution its power and definition?

The U.S. Constitution at Article III Sec. 2 Paragraph 2 states "In all Cases affecting Ambassadors, other public Ministers and Consuls, and those in which a State shall be Party, the Supreme Court shall have original Jurisdiction."

The city, county, or State is not following the U.S. Constitution when they have citizens brought before a municipal, county or state court in the name of the State. When you ask questions to those concerning this issue, ask them to show you the law which overrules the U.S. Constitution. They will not be able to do this because there is not such state law that overrules the Constitution.

Section 241 of Title 18 is the civil rights conspiracy statute. Section 241 makes it unlawful for two or more persons to agree together to injure, threaten, or intimidate a person in any state, territory or district in the free exercise or enjoyment of any right or privilege secured to him/her by the Constitution or the laws of the Unites States, (or because of his/her having exercised the same). Unlike most conspiracy statutes, Section 241 does not require that one of the conspirators commit an overt act prior to the conspiracy becoming a crime.

If two or more persons conspire to injure, oppress, threaten, or intimidate any person in any State, Territory, Commonwealth, Possession, or District in the free exercise or enjoyment of any right or privilege secured to him by the Constitution or laws of the United States, or because of his having so exercised the same;... They shall be fined under this title or imprisoned not more than ten years, or both; and if death results from the acts committed in violation of this section or if such acts include kidnapping or an attempt to kidnap, aggravated sexual abuse or an attempt to commit aggravated sexual abuse, or an attempt to kill, they shall be fined under this title or imprisoned for any term of years or for life, or both, or may be sentenced to death.

Section 242 of Title 18 makes it a crime for a person acting under color of any law to willfully deprive a person of a right or privilege protected by the Constitution or laws of the United States.

For the purpose of Section 242, acts under "color of law" include acts not only done by federal, state, or local officials within the their lawful authority, but also acts done beyond the bounds of that official's lawful authority, if the acts are done while the official is purporting to or pretending to act in the performance of his/her official duties. Persons acting under color of law within the meaning of this statute include police officers, prisons guards and other law enforcement officials, as well as judges, care providers in public health facilities, and others who are acting as public officials. It is not necessary that the crime be motivated by animus toward the race, color, religion, sex, handicap, familial status or national origin of the victim.

Whoever, under color of any law, statute, ordinance, regulation, or custom, willfully subjects any person in any State, Territory, Commonwealth, Possession, or District to the deprivation of any rights, privileges, or immunities secured or protected by the Constitution or laws of the United States, ... shall be fined under this title or imprisoned not more than one year, or both; and if bodily injury results from the acts committed in violation of this section or if such acts include the use, attempted use, or threatened use of a dangerous weapon, explosives, or fire, shall be fined under this title or imprisoned not more than ten years, or both; and if death results from the acts committed in violation of this section or if such acts include kidnapping or an attempt to kidnap, aggravated sexual abuse, or an attempt to commit aggravated sexual abuse, or an attempt to kill, shall be fined under this title, or imprisoned for any term of years or for life, or both, or may be sentenced to death.

"An action by Department of Motor Vehicles, whether directly or through a court sitting administratively as the hearing officer, must be clearly defined in the statute before it has subject matter jurisdiction, without such jurisdiction of the licensee, all acts of the agency, by its employees, agents, hearing officers, are null and void." Doolan v. Carr, 125 US 618; City v Pearson, 181 Cal. 640.

"Agency, or party sitting for the agency, (which would be the magistrate of a municipal court) has no authority to enforce as to any licensee unless he is acting for compensation. Such an act is highly penal in nature, and should not be construed to include anything which is not embraced within its terms. Where there is no charge within a complaint that the accused was employed for compensation to do the act complained of, or that the act constituted part of a contract." Schomig v. Kaiser, 189 Cal 596.

"When acting to enforce a statute and its subsequent amendments to the present date, the Judge of the municipal court is acting as an administrative officer and not in a judicial capacity; courts in administering or enforcing statutes do not act judicially, but merely ministerially". Thompson v. Smith, 154 SE 583.

"A Judge ceases to sit as a judicial officer because the governing principle of administrative law provides that courts are prohibited from substituting their evidence, testimony, record, arguments, and rationale for that of the agency. Additionally, courts are prohibited from substituting their judgment for that of the agency. Courts in administrative issues are prohibited from even listening to or hearing arguments, presentation, or rational." ASIS v. US, 568 F2d 284.

"Ministerial officers are incompetent to receive grants of judicial power from the legislature; their acts in attempting to exercise such powers are necessarily nullities." Burns v. Sup. Ct., SF, 140 Cal. 1.

"The elementary doctrine that the constitutionality of a legislative act is open to attack only by persons whose rights are affected thereby, applies to statute relating to administrative agencies, the validity of which may not be called into question in the absence of a showing of substantial harm, actual or impending, to a legally protected interest directly resulting from the enforcement of the statute." Board of Trade v. Olson, 262 US 1; 29 ALR 2d 105.

We all have been programmed to believe that when the state makes a law it is supreme, however state law does not overrule the U.S. Constitution. State officials want you to believe this as it produces more income for them and of course less effort for them to collect money from you. As long as the top elected officials can keep everyone programmed to believe they are just doing their job they have nothing to worry about except how much money they will get upon retirement and how much they can get before retirement.

The U.S. Supreme Court has become so corrupt and despotic that they only take and rule on cases that they want to hear. Does this sound Constitutional within reason or common sense logic?

Why don't they follow the Law of the land, the U.S. Constitution? The reason is very clear. They are all corrupt and want more of your money.

The courts justices decide what cases will be published in the law books. When a case comes along that is detrimental to the court or its justices, they simply discard it and refuse to have it published in the law journals.

When you swear before God to uphold the U.S. Constitution, you have taken an oath that someday you are going to be accountable for. The spirit world knows everything and nobody gets away with anything. All karma must be balanced with dharma. Vengeance is God's and he will repay. An eye for an eye and a tooth for a tooth.

Noah Webster stated in his early edition dictionary that the word accountable means liable to be called to account; answerable to a superior; as every man is accountable to God for his conduct. Of course you won't find this true definition in any of the up to date Noah Webster's dictionary's as our government has changed the definition to exclude the true meaning and the word of God.

"The institutions of our society are founded on the belief that there is an authority higher than the authority of the state; that there is a moral law which the state is powerless to alter; that the individual possesses rights, conferred by the creator, which government must respect." McGowan v. Maryland, 366 U.S. 520, S. Ct. 1961

The words ignorance of the Law is no excuse. It comes from the civil law of the Romans on which state law is made. The civil law of the state requires a law to be written and put on display. The Roman Emperor Caligula had his laws written very small and hung so high up that no one could read them. He used these laws to imprison, kill, fine, and destroy people, who believe that he is not the God of the state. The majority of these were Christians.

The same thing is happening now in the U.S.A. Since there are so many state laws which are written so the average man can understand them, even if he could ever read them all.

Questions to ask police officers about stops:

Did you know the definition of driving is a commercial act, as in operating the motor vehicle?

Did you know a motor vehicle is defined as a taxi, omnibus, or any variety of motor vehicles exclusively used and designed for commerce?

Did you know no State shall convert a liberty to a privilege, license it, and attach a fee to it? Murdock v. Penn., 319 U.S. 105 1943

Did you know if the State converts a liberty into a privilege, the Citizen can engage in the right with impunity? Shuttlesworth v. Birmingham, 373 U.S. 262 1963

Did you know a pretextual traffic stop is violation of the 4th amendment of the U.S. Constitution?

U.S. v. Eldridge, 984 F. 2d 934 (8th Cir. 1993)

Did you know a valid investigated stop must be based on reasonable articulable suspicion?

U.S. v. Briggman, 931 F. 2d 705 (11th Cir. 1991);

U.S. v. Strickland, 902 F. 2d 937 (11th Cir. 1990);

U.S. v. Stranhan, 984 F. 2d 155 (6th Cir. 1993).

Did you know your questions must relate to the purpose of the stop or detention of the driver is unreasonable? U.S. v. Barahona, 990 F. 2d 412 (8th Cir. 1993)

Did you know that all persons have a God given Right and a Constitutional secured Right to refuse to give you and information and/or confirm their Identity even though you have a probable cause to stop them?

"Probable cause is not established either by failing to represent identification upon request by law enforcement officers or by carrying a plastic bag in one's travel luggage, USCA Constitution Amendment 4." People are entitled to refuse to provide information to the police. USCA Constitution

5th. Cesar Moya v. United States, 761 mF. 2d 322 (7th Cir. 1985); United States v. Brown 731 F. 2d 1491 (11th Cir. 1984); Brown v. Texas, 443 U.S. 47 (7th Cir. 1979).

Did you know you have no authority to arrest anyone solely to ascertain their identity? Arrington v. McDonald, 808 F. 2d 466, (6th Cir. 1986).

Did you know refusing consent of a search is not bases for reason of suspicion, supporting detention, nor probable cause, to search or impound my vehicle. U.S. v. Manuel, 992 F. 2d 272 (10th Cir. 1993).

Did you know refusing consent does not establish probable cause to search a vehicle? U.S. v. Alexander, 835 F. 2d 1406 (11th Cir. 1993).

Did you know once documentation is returned, I am free to go? U.S. v. Soro, 988 F. 2d 1548 (10th Cir. 1993); Parker v. Strong, 717 F. Supp. 767 (1989)

Searches and Seizures:

The fact that the police officer was performing a community care taking function, cannot itself justify warrant less search of private residence. U.S. v. Erickson, 991 F. 2d 529 (9th Cir. 1993).

Individuals need not have to be accused of wrong doing to enjoy the protections of the 4th Amendment. Cassady v. Tackett, 938 F. 2d 693 (6th Cir. 1990)

Even if my vehicle was stopped legitimately, the police may not search it without probable cause. U.S. v. Wanless, 882 F. 2d 1459 (9th Cir. 1989) Unlawful search and seizure, your rights must be interpreted in favor of the Citizen. Byars v. U.S., 372 U.S. 28, 33 (1927) Police officers did not have probable cause to arrest passengers for giving false information, resulting in search of this person.

A frisk may only pat for weapons, not reaching in pockets. Officers must first believe that a threat is poised. U.S. v. Santillanes, 848 F. 2d 1103 (10th Cir. 1988); U.S. v. Wanless, 882 F. 2d 1459 (9th Cir. 1989) Government must prove alleged consent to search, and that consent was given freely and voluntarily.

U.S. v. Villarreal, 963 F. 2d 770 (5th Cir. 1992) Government must prove consent to search by preponderance of evidence. U.S. v. Tillman, 963 F. 2d 137 (6th Cir. 1992) Consent to search must be proved by clear and positive testimony and must be unequivocally, specified and intelligently given, uncontaminated by any duress and coercion. Waivers of rights must be done knowing and voluntary. White v. White, 925 F. 2d 287 (9th Cir. 1991)

Having a large amount of cash is not per se evidence of drug related illegal activity for forfeiture purposes. U.S. v. $31,990 in U.S. Currency, 982 F 2d 851 (2nd Cir. 1993). U.S. v. $124,570 in U.S. Currency, 873 2 Fd 1240 (9th Cir. 1889)

Court is not empowered to suspend constitutional guarantees so that government can fight war on drugs more effectively. USCA Constitutional Amendment 4., U.S. Of A., Appellee, v. Jose Luis Garcia, appellant, Eight Circuit, #93-2195, 93-2634, decided May 4, 1994. "The Claim and exercise of a Constitutional right cannot be converted into a crime," Miller v. U.S., F. 2d 486, 489.

"The right of the citizen to travel upon the public highways and to transport his property thereon, either by horse drawn carriage or by automobile, is not a mere privilege which a city may prohibit at will, but a common right which he has under the right to life, liberty, and the pursuit of happiness." Thompson v. Smith, 154 SE 579. The right to travel is a part of the liberty of which the citizen cannot be deprived without due process of law under the 5th Amendment. Kend v. Dulles, 357 US 116, 125. Government, in restricting and blocking highways and roadways for vehicle inspections and license checks are violating the people's common law right to travel.

When used in this chapter the term - ... 'Motor vehicle' means every description of carriage or other contrivance propelled or drawn by mechanical power and used for commercial purposes on the highways in the transportation of passengers, passengers and property, or property or cargo; 18 USC Sec. 31

Traffic – Commerce; trade; sale or exchange of merchandise, bills, money, and the like. The passing or exchange of goods or commodities from one person to another for an equivalent in goods or money. The subjects of transportation on a route, as persons or goods …

Passengers:

The fact that a person is in the company of a person for whom a warrant has been issued does not constitute probable cause for search of that person. U.S. v. Prieto-Villa, 910 F. 2d 601 (9th Cir. 1990) mere presences/association with possessor of contraband is insufficient to establish possession on my part.

U.S. v. Garcia, 983 F. 2d 1160 (1st Cir. 1993) Mere presence or association with another who possessed contraband is insufficient to establish constructive possession. It is not a crime simply to travel with, even knowingly, someone who is carrying drugs; U.S. v. Teffera, 985 F. 2d 1082 (D.C. Cir. 1993) Association with criminals by proximity, conversation, or companionship is insufficient to support probable cause to arrest; U.S. v. Munoz, 738 F. Supp. 800 (1990)

Arrest:

Arrest may not be used as a pretext for a search; Laing v. U.S., 8981 F. 2d 683 (8th Cir. 1989); arrest may not be used as a pretext to search for evidence; search must have at least some relation to matter and purpose of arrest. Arrest must be both custodial and lawful to support a "search incident to arrest", U.S. v. Mota, 982 F. 2d 1384 (9th Cir. 1993) A search incident to arrest is limited to area within my immediate control (not entire car if cuffed at rear); U.S. v. Vasey, 834 F 2d 782 (9th Cir. 1987); U.S. v. Hernandez, 901 F 2d 1217 (5th Cir. 1990), Although license plate violation provided probable cause to arrest driver of tractor trailer truck, violation alone did not provide probable cause to search the trailer compartment. I may verbally challenge the officer's actions to demand I.D.; Gainor v. Rogers, 973 F 2d 1379 (8th Cir. 1992), 1st Amendment protects arrestee's rights to verbally challenge police officers action in asking for I.D.

Police supervisors are liable if they authorize or approve unconstitutional conduct of offending officers, White v. Farrier, 849 F 2d 322 (8th Cir. 1988).

Supervisory personnel are subject to liability where evidence establishes that they authorized or approved unconstitutional conduct of the offending officers, Gandhi v. Detroit Police Dept., 747 F 2d 338 (6th Cir. 1984); Stokes v. Delcambre, 710 F 2d 1120 (5th Cir 1983) A federal officer who uses excessive force is not acting in good faith and may be resisted, U.S. v. Span, 970 F 2d 573 (9th Cir. 1992), Under 4th Amendment, person had right to be free from use of excessive force by law enforcement officer even when that officer is making lawful arrest.

For an arrest to be valid under the 4th Amendment, probable cause must exist. Funnaway v. New York, 445 US 573, (1980) Courts must be especially cautious when the evidence that is alleged to establish probable cause is entirely consistent with innocent behavior. Reid v. Georgia, 448 US. 438, 65 L. Ed. 2d 890, 100 S. Ct. 2752 (1980) People stopped at a traffic road block are usually going to and from work, to the grocery store, or some other innocent behavior. Moya v. U.S. 761 F 2d 322, (7th Cir. 1985); Brown v. Texas, 433 US 47, 61 L. Ed. 2d 357. 99 S. Ct. 2637 (1979). The Constitution protects individuals against invasion of their privacy by the Government. Rimie v. City of Hedwig Village, Texas, 765 F. 2d 490 (1985); Whalen v. Roe, 429 US 589, 51 L. Ed. 2d 64, 97 S. Ct. 869 (1977); Blocking off highways for license checks is invading the expectation of privacy of each driver without probable cause. This with someone knowledgeable of their Constitutional rights would bring a lawsuit against the officer in his official and individual capacity. The officer will have to hire an attorney to represent him as his department will be unable to represent him as it will be a conflict of interest. Monell v. Department of Social Services of the City of New York. Local governments were persons under Title 42 USC Sec. 1983. Meaning that a local unit could be sued directly for unconstitutional acts implementing or executing a policy, ordinance, regulation, or decision officially adopted and promulgated by it. Liability could arise for unconstitutional actions obedient to governmental customs with the force of law, even though such actions had not received formal approval through a local unit's official decision making process. Enforcement of unconstitutional policies or customs made by those who edicts or acts may fairly be said to represent official policy could result in local government liability. This decision also permits suits against officers held in their official rather than person capacities, thereby providing another way to recover payment of damages from the local unit itself.

Probable Cause:

Unless there is some special exception, all containers and packages will receive the full protection of the 4th Amendment during a police search, US v.Bonitz, 826 F 2d 954 (1987). Warrant less search of a grocery bag which provided probable cause for arrest, held not justified incident to arrest, U.S. v. Most, 876 F 2d 191 (D.C. Cir. 1989), The passenger has a standing to challenge the constitutionality of a vehicle stop giving that the stop results in the seizure of the passenger. Jackson v. Vannoy 49 F 3d 175 (5th Cir. 1995). Even the passenger has standing to sue for the illegal stop, the government bears the entire burden of proving by preponderance of evidence that consent to the search was freely and voluntarily given. US v. Saadeh 61 F 3d 510 (7th Cir. 1995) The 4th Amendment does not allow random searches of persons traveling the nations highways. Karnes v. Skrutski, 62 F. 3d 485 (3rd Cir. 1995) Consent encounters and searches are valid only if the suspects consent was freely and voluntarily given. US v. Nobles 69 F 3d 172 (1995) A warrant must be gotten and must particularly describe the place, the person to be search, and the person or things to be sees to be valid. US v. Layne 43 F 3d 127 (5th Cir. 1995) Absent exigent circumstances, police officers may not undertake warrant less search, US v. Biggs, 70 F 3d 913 (6th Cir. 1995). Unlawful search can never be justified by its fruits, Parkhurst v. Trapp, 77 F 3d 707 (3rd Cir. 1996).

Building more prisons and hiring more police officers will not restrict crime as history can verify this. Teaching children right from wrong is the only way to stop crime. Hiring more police and special task force's will never curb crime, but will certainly continue to alienate millions of Americans from a government that they no longer recognize as their own. Absent exigent circumstances or consent, officer is not to search lock suitcases without a search warrant. Florida v. Wells, 495 US 1 (1990) Unless exigent circumstances exist, warrant searches are impermissible. US v. Almont, 952 F 2d 20 (1st Cir. 1991)

Situations that demand unusual or immediate action in relation to justification for warrant less arrests or search refers generally to those situations in which law enforcement agents will be unable or likely to effectuate and arrest, search or seizure for which probable cause exists unless they act swiftly and without seeking prior judicial authorization. Search warrants must describe both the place to be searched and things to be seized with particularity, US v. Brown 984 F 2d 1074 (10th Cir. 1993).

If there is no warrant for road blocks and check lanes, exercising the right to refuse consent to search cannot alone be basis of reasonable suspicion supporting detention of suspect, US v. Manuel, 992 F 2d 272 (1993), Excessive force during arrest violates a persons 4th Amendment Right against unreasonable searches and seizures, Swoboda v. Dubach, 992 F. 2d 186 (10th Cir. 1993). Probable cause to arrest does not automatically provide probable cause to search, US v. Jones, 994 F 2d 1051 (3rd Cir. 1993), Police may not search without a warrant, US v. Parra, 2 F 3d 1058 (1993); Peyton v. New York, 445 US 573 (1980).

The 4th Amendment protects expectations of privacy in moveable closed containers, and that includes automobiles unless you have a warrant. US v. Gooch 6 F 3d 673 (9th Cir. 1993), Police themselves cannot create exigent circumstances such that warrant requirements will be suspended under exigent circumstances exception, US v. Halliman, 923 F 2d 873 (D.C. Cir. 1991), Government has the burden of proof "consent" to search by a preponderance of the evidence, US v Hodge 19 F 3d 51 (1994), Because interrogation and search were direct result of illegal traffic stop, all evidence had to be stricken or suppressed, US v. Millam, 36 F 3d 886 (1994), A search by government agents is presumptively unreasonable under the 4th Amendment unless conducted pursuant to warrant issued by judicial officer upon finding of probable cause, US v. Warren, 42 F 3d 647 (1994), Suspicion is not such "reasonable suspicion" as will justify investigatory stop if it is not more than inchoate and unparticularized or "hunch", US v. Garcia, 23 F 3d 1331 (1994). Terry v. Ohio, 392 US 1 (1968) states, "For an investigative stop to be valid there must be articulable suspicion before you may stop and search".

Trezevant V. City of Tampa 741 F 2d 336 (11th Cir. 1984) Motorist illegally held for 23 minutes on a traffic charge was awarded $25,000 in damages.

Bivens v. Six Unknown Named Agents, 403 U.S. 388 (1971), was a case in which the United States Supreme Court ruled that an implied cause of action existed for an individual whose 4th Amendment freedom from unreasonable search and seizures had been violated by federal agents. The victim of such a deprivation could sue for the violation of the Amendment itself, despite the lack of any federal statute authorizing such a suit. The existence of a remedy for the violation was implied from the importance of the right violated.

Bivens has been subsequently interpreted to create a cause of action against the federal government similar to the one 42 U.S.C. § 1983 creates against the states.

Hafer v. Melo, 502 U.S. 21, 25-31 (1991), states the U.S. Supreme Court held that State officers are subject to § 1983 liability for damages in their personal capacities, even when the conduct in question relates to their official duties. You can sue Government agents.

Justice Sandra Day O'Connor, writing for a unanimous 8-0 court, wrote that:

In Will v. Michigan Dept. of State Police, 491 U.S. 58, 105 L. Ed. 2d 45, 109 S. Ct. 2304 (1989), we held that state officials "acting in their official capacities" are outside the class of "persons" subject to liability under Rev. Stat. § 1979, 42 U.S.C. § 1983. 491 U.S. at 71. Petitioner takes this language to mean that § 1983 does not authorize suits against state officers for damages arising from official acts. We reject this reading of Will and hold that state officials sued in their individual capacities are "persons" for purposes of § 1983.

Government official must take the oath to get paid.

U.S. Code: Title 2, Chapter 3. § 35. Salaries payable monthly after taking oath - Each Member and Delegate, after he has taken and subscribed the required oath, is entitled to receive his salary at the end of each month.

U.S. Code: Title 5, Part III, Subpart B, Chapter 33, Subchapter II, § 3331. Oath of office - An individual, except the President, elected or appointed to an office of honor or profit in the civil service or uniformed services, shall take the following oath: "I, _____, do solemnly swear (or affirm) that I will support and defend the Constitution of the United States against all enemies, foreign and domestic; that I will bear true faith and allegiance to the same; that I take this obligation freely, without any mental reservation or purpose of evasion; and that I will well and faithfully discharge the duties of the office on which I am about to enter. So help me God." This section does not affect other oaths required by law.

U.S. Code: Title 18, Part I, Chapter 13, § 242. Deprivation of rights under color of law - Whoever, under color of any law, statute, ordinance, regulation, or custom, willfully subjects any person in any State, Territory, Commonwealth, Possession, or District to the deprivation of any rights, privileges, or immunities secured or protected by the Constitution or laws of the United States, or to different punishments, pains, or penalties, on account of such person being an alien, or by reason of his color, or race, than are prescribed for the punishment of citizens, shall be fined under this title or imprisoned not more than one year, or both; and if bodily injury results from the acts committed in violation of this section or if such acts include the use, attempted use, or threatened use of a dangerous weapon, explosives, or fire, shall be fined under this title or imprisoned not more than ten years, or both; and if death results from the acts committed in violation of this section or if such acts include kidnapping or an attempt to kidnap, aggravated sexual abuse, or an attempt to commit aggravated sexual abuse, or an attempt to kill, shall be fined under this title, or imprisoned for any term of years or for life, or both, or may be sentenced to death.

"Waivers of constitutional rights not only must be voluntary but must be knowing, intelligent acts done with sufficient awareness of the relevant circumstances and likely consequences." Brady vs. US, 397 US 742; 90 S.Ct. 1463 (May 4, 1970)

Other Court Cases:
- Davis v. Mississippi – Fingerprints are personal property and you do not have to surrender them.
- Privacy Protection Act 1974 – Unauthorized police radio call-ins for background checks on people are illegal.
-

"Countries are well cultivated, not as they are fertile, but as they are free. There is no cruder tyranny than that which is perpetuated under the shield of law and in the name of justice." Charles De Secondat, Baron De Montesquieu

LAND PATENTS AND ALLODIAL TITLES

American Insurance Co. et al., The v. Canter (356 Bales of Cotton) 1 Pet. 511, 7 L.Ed 242 (1828)

"The Constitution and laws of the United States give jurisdiction to the District Courts, over all cases in admiralty; but jurisdiction over the cases, does not constitute the case itself."

"The Constitution declares that "the judicial power shall extend to all cases in law and equity arising under it – the laws of the United States, and treaties made, or which shall be made under their authority; to all cases affecting ambassadors, other public ministers and consuls; to all cases of admiralty and maritime jurisdiction." The Constitution certainly contemplates these as three distinct classes of cases; and if they are distinct, the grant of jurisdiction over one of them does not confer jurisdiction over either of the other two. The discrimination made between them is conclusive against their identity."

"Although admiralty jurisdiction can be exercised in the States, in those courts only which are established in pursuance of the third article of the Constitution, the same limitation does not extend to the territories."

"Nor do I doubt that the admiralty jurisdiction over revenue cases, as exercised by the Kentucky court, is rightfully vested (and that beyond the control of the Florida Legislature) in the Superior Court of this district."

"But here, it appears to me, the grant of jurisdiction terminates. The admiralty jurisdiction, beyond this limit, is left to be administered under the laws of the territory, for this simple reason, that other causes occurring in the admiralty, cannot be brought within this description of causes, arising under the laws of the United States…."

"The 5th section of the act of 1823 creates a territorial Legislature, which shall have legislative powers over all rightful objects of legislation; but no law shall be valid which is inconsistent with the laws and Constitution of the Unites States."

"The Constitution and laws of the Unites States give jurisdiction to the District Courts over all cases in admiralty; but jurisdiction over the case does not constitute the case itself. We are therefore to inquire, whether cases in admiralty, and cases arising under the laws and Constitution of the United States, are identical."

"If we have recourse to that pure fountain from which all the jurisdiction of the federal courts is derived, we find language employed which cannot well be misunderstood. The Constitution declares, that the judicial power shall extend to all cases in law and equity, arising under this Constitution, the laws of the United States, and treaties made, or which shall be made under their authority; to all cases affecting ambassadors, or other public ministers, and consuls; to all cases of admiralty and maritime jurisdiction."

The Constitution certainly contemplates these as three distinct classes of cases, and if they are distinct, the grant of jurisdiction over one of them does not confer jurisdiction over either of the other two. The discrimination made between them, in the Constitution, is, we think, conclusive against their identity. If it were not so – if this were a point open to inquiry – it would be difficult to maintain the proposition that they are the same. A case in admiralty does not, in fact, arise under the Constitution or laws of the United States. These cases are as old as navigation itself; and the law, admiralty and maritime, as it has existed for ages, is applied by our courts to the cases as they arise. It is not, then, to the 8th section of the territorial law that we are to look for the grant of admiralty and maritime jurisdiction to the territorial courts. Consequently, if that jurisdiction is exclusive, it is not made so by the reference to the District Court of Kentucky."

"It has been contended, that by the Constitution the judicial power of the United States extends to all cases of admiralty and maritime jurisdiction, and that the whole of this judicial power must be vested "in one Supreme Court, and in such inferior courts as Congress shall from time to time ordain and establish." Hence it has been argued, that Congress cannot vest admiralty jurisdiction in courts created by the territorial Legislature."

"We have only to pursue this subject one step further, to perceive that this provision of the Constitution does not apply to it. The next sentence declares that "the judges both of the supreme and inferior courts shall hold their offices during good behavior." The judges of the Superior Courts of Florida hold their offices for four years. These courts, then, are not Constitutional courts, in which the judicial power conferred by the Constitution on the general government can be deposited. They are incapable of receiving it. They are legislative courts, created in virtue of the general right of sovereignty which exists in the government, or in virtue of that clause which enables Congress to make all needful rules and regulations, respecting the territory belonging to the United States. The jurisdiction with which they are invested, is not a part of that judicial power which is defined in Article III of the Constitution, but is conferred by Congress, in the execution of those general powers which that body possesses over the territories of the United States. Although admiralty jurisdiction can be exercised in the States in those courts only which are established in pursuance of Article III of the Constitution, the same limitation does not extend to the territories. In legislating for them, Congress exercises the combined powers of the general and of a State government."

Cleveland v. Smith, 132 U.S. 318 "Neither a town nor its officers have any right to appropriate or interfere with private property.

Johnson v. Christian, 128 U.S. 374 (1888)
Marshall v. Ladd, 7 Wall. (74 U.S.) 106 (1869)

McGarrahan v. Mining Co., 96 U.S. 316 (1877)
1. The statutory provisions prescribing the manner in which a patent of the United States for land shall be executed are mandatory. No equivalent for any of the required formalities is allowed, but each of the integral acts to be performed is essential to the perfection and validity of such an instrument. If, therefore, it is not actually countersigned by the recorder of the General Land Office in person or, in his absence, by the principal clerk of private land claims as acting recorder, it is not executed according to law and does not pass the title of the United States.
2. The record in the volume kept for that purpose at the General Land Office at Washington of a patent which has been executed in the manner which the law directs is evidence of the same dignity and is subject to the same defenses as the patent itself. If the instrument, as the same appears of record, was not so executed and was therefore insufficient on its face to transfer the title of the United States, the record raises no presumption that a patent duly executed was delivered to and accepted by the grantee.
3. The Act of March 3, 1843, 5 Stat. 627, in relation to exemplifications of records, does not dispense with the provisions of law touching the signing and countersigning. The record, to prove a valid

patent, must still show that they were complied with. The names need not be fully inserted in the record, but it must appear in some form that they were actually signed to the patent when it was issued.

4. The failure to record a patent does not defeat the grant. This was ejectment by William McGarrahan in the District Court of the Twentieth Judicial District of California in and for Santa Clara County against the New Idria Mining Company to recover possession of certain lands in that state known as the Rancho Panoche Grande. He claimed them under a patent therefore which he alleged had been issued by the United States to Vicente P. Gomez, his grantor, under the act of Congress to (Page 96 U. S. 317) ascertain and settle the private land claims in the State of California, approved March 3, 1851, 9 Stat. 631. The patent was not produced upon the trial, but the plaintiff put in evidence a certified copy of an instrument as the same was recorded in a volume kept at the General Land Office at Washington for the recording of patents of the United States for confirmed Mexican land grants in California, being volume 4 of such records, upon pages 312-321 inclusive. The concluding portion of that copy is as follows: "In testimony whereof, I, Abraham Lincoln, President of the United States, have caused these letters to be made patent, and the seal of the General Land Office to be hereunto affixed." "Given under my hand at the City of Washington, this fourteenth day of March, in the year of our Lord one thousand eight hundred and sixty three, and of the independence of the United States the eighty seventh."

"[L. S.] By the President: Abraham Lincoln"
"By W. O. Stoddard"
"Secretary"
"Acting Recorder of the General Land Office"

As the only question decided by this court is whether the exemplification admitted on the trial of the cause shows upon its face the execution of a patent sufficient in law to pass the title of the United States, no reference is made to the other points which arose in the court below and were elaborately discussed by counsel here. The district court rendered judgment for the defendant, which was affirmed by the Supreme Court. McGarrahan then sued out this writ of error. (Page 96 U. S. 318)

Peck v. Jenness, 48 U.S. 7 How. 612 612 (1849)

Summa Corp. v. Calif. St. Lands Comm. U.S., 80 80 L.Ed. 237, 104 S.Ct. 1751; USSC 82-708.

United States v. Cherokee Nation, 474 F.2d 628, 634 (1973).

United States v. Creek Nation, 295 U.S. 103, 111 (1935)

Wallace v. Harmstad, S Ct 492 (1863).

Wilcox v. Jackson, 43 Peter (U.S.) 498, 10 L Ed. 264

Wright v Mattison, 18 How. (U.S.) 50 (1855).

SECTION IV
THE UNITED STATES OF AMERICA
A REPUBLIC UNDER GOD
LAND PATENTS, EJECTMENT, AND ESTOPPEL

1. In case of ejectment, where the question is who has the legal title, the patent of the government is unassailable. Sanford v. Sanford, 139 US 642.

2. The transfer of legal title (patent) to public domain gives the transferee the right to possess and enjoy the land transferred. Gibson v. Chouteau, 80 US 92.

3. A patent for land is the highest evidence of title and is conclusive as against the government and all claiming under junior patents or titles. United States v. Stone, 2 US 525.

4. The presumption being that it (patent) is valid and passes the legal title. Minter v. Crommelin, 18 US 87.

5. Estoppels have been sustained as against a municipal corporation (county), Beadle v. Smyser, 209 US 393.

6. A court of law will not uphold or enforce an equitable title to land as a defense to an action of ejectment. Johnson v. Christian, 128 US 374, Doe v. Aiken, 31 F. 393.

7. When congress has prescribed the conditions upon which portions of the public domain may be alienated (to convey, to transfer), and has provided that upon the fulfillment of the conditions the United States shall issue a patent to the purchaser, then such land is not taxable by a state. Sargent v Herrick & Stevens, 221 US 404, Northern P.R. CO. v. Trail County, 115 US 600.

8. The patent alone passes land from the United States to the grantee and nothing passes a perfect title to public lands but a patent. Wilcox v. Jackson, 13 Peter (US) 498.

9. Patents and other evidences of title from the United States government are not controlled by state recording laws and shall be effective, as against subsequent purchasers, only from the time of their record in the county. Lomax v. Pickering, 173 US 26.

10. In federal courts the patent is held to be the foundation of title at law. Fenn v. Holmes, 21 Howard 481.

11. Congress has the sole power to declare the dignity and effect of titles emanating from the United States and the whole legislation of the government, in reference to the public lands, declare the patent to be the superior and conclusive evidence of the legal title. Until it issues, the fee is in the Government, which by the patent passes to the grantee, and he is entitled to enforce the possession in ejectment. Bagnell v. Broderick. 13 Peter (US) 450.

12. In ejectment the legal title must prevail, and a patent of the United States to public lands pass that title: it can not be assailed collaterally on the ground that false and perjured testimony was used to secure it. Steel v. St. Louis Smelting and Refining Co., 106 US 417.

13. A patent certificate, or patent issued, or confirmation made to an original grantee or his legal representatives of the grantee or assignee by contract, as well as by law. Hogan v. Pace, 69 US 605.

14. In federal courts, the rule that ejectment cannot be maintained on a mere equitable title is strictly enforced, so that ejectment cannot be maintained on a mere entry made with a register and receiver, but only on the patent, since the certificates of the officers of the land department vest in the locator only equitable title, This rule prevails in the federal courts even when the statute of the state in

which the suit is brought provides that a receipt from the local land office is sufficient proof of title to support the action. Langdon v. Sherwood, 124 U.S. 74, Carter v. Ruddy, 166 US 493.

15. The plaintiff in ejectment must in all cases prove the legal title to the premises in himself, at the time of the demise laid in the declaration, and evidence of an equitable title will not be sufficient for a recovery. The practice of allowing ejectment to be maintained in state courts upon equitable titles cannot affect the jurisdiction of the courts of the United States. Fenn v. Holmes, 21 Howard 41.

16. Under USCA Constitution, Article 4, section 3, clause 2, Congress, in exercise of its discretion in disposal of public lands, had power, by this section, to restrict alienation of homestead lands after conveyance by United states in fee simple, by providing no, such lands shall become liable to satisfaction of debts contracted prior to issuance of patent. Ruddy v. Rossi, (1918) 248 US 104.

17. Patents are tied to the Bible, in Genesis 47 by way of the word assigned in italicized print. Also note in later verses the beginning of sharecropping, BC 1701.

18. The right to the ownership of property and to contract with respect of its use is unalienable. Golding v. Schubac, 93 U.S. 32: Saville v. Corless, 46 U.S. 495.

19. Parties in possession of real property have the right to stand on their possessions until compelled to yield to the rule title determined by trial by jury. 47 Am. Jur. 2d 45.20. Giving a note does not constitute payment. Echart v. Commissioners, I.R.S. 42 F2d 158; 283 U.S. 140.

20. Actual or threatened exercise of power over the property of another is coercion and duress which will render the payment involuntary. Cleveland v. Richardson, 132 US 318.

21. Property value means the price the property will command in the market, or its equivalent in lawful money. People v. Hines, 89 P. 858. 5 Cal. App. 122

22. Neither a town nor its officers have any right to appropriate or interfere with private property. Mitchell v. City of Rockland, 46 Me. 496.

23. A state may provide for the collection of taxes in gold and silver only, State Treasurer v. Wright, 28 ILL. 509: Whitaker v. Haley, 2 Ore. 128.

24. Taxes lawfully assessed, are collectible by agents in money and notes, cannot be accepted in payment. Town of Frankfort v. Waldo, 128 Me. 1.

25. There must be strict compliance with statutory requirements to divest property owners of their property titles for non payment of taxes. McCarthy v. Greenlawn Cem., 168 Me. 388 (1962).

26. At common law there was no tax lien. Cassidy v. Aroostook, 134 Me. 341 (1936).

27. A tax on real estate to one not the owner is not valid.
Barker v Blake, 36 Me. 433 (1853).

1807 – 2 Stat. 437, 9th Cong. Sess. II, Ch. 31
1807 – 2 Stat. 437, 9th Cong. Sess. II, Ch. 37
1810 – The Act to Estab. General Land Off. in Dept. of Treasury 2 Stat. 590, 11th Cong. Sess. II. Ch 35
1812 – Major Land Patent Stat. to Dispose of Lands 2 Stat. 748, 12th Cong. Sess.I, Ch. 99
1812 – 2 Stat. 748, 12th Cong. Sess. I, Ch. 77

1812 – 2 Stat. 748, 12th Cong. Sess.I, Ch 68
1820 – 3 Stat. 716, 12th Cong. Sess.I Ch. 51
1824 – 5 Stat. 566, 16th Cong. Sess.I, Ch. 174
1824 – 5 Stat. 51, 18th Cong. Sess.I. Ch. 174
1824 – 5 Stat. 52, 18th Cong. Sess.I Ch. 172
1831 – 5 Stat. 56, 21st Cong. Sess. II Ch. 30
1847 – Act to Raise Additional Military Forces & other purposes 8 Stat. 123, 29th Cong. Sess. II Ch. 8
1850 – Military Bounty Service Act 9 Stat. 520 31st Cong. Sess. I. Ch. 85
1862 – The Homestead Act Sect. 4 12 Stat. 392, 37th Cong. Sess. II Ch. 75
1864 – October 31st, Pres. Proc. by Abe Lincoln on Equal Footing Doctrine w/States
1864 – Ch. XXXVI of 12 united States Statutes at Large, Equal Footing in All Aspects

33 Am. Jur. 419, Sect. 2
40 Am. Jur. 577-688,
42 Am. Jur. Sec. 781-873
47 Am Jur. 2d 45,
51 Am. Jur. Sect. 20 & 21

The Supreme Court Digests on Land patents
43 USCS 17
Committee for Economic Development – Adaptive Program for Agriculture/seize
10,000 farms
1 Kent Commentaries, 471
Vatican II Project
Treaty of 1783
The Great Turtle Land Treaty – Haudusance Nations
Northwest Ordinance of 1787
Treaty of Peace, 8 Stat. 80 of 1783
Treaty of Ghent, 8 Stat. 218 1818
Oregon Treaty, 9 Stat. 869 June 15, 1846
Treaty of Guadalupe Hidalgo, 9 Stat. 922 1848
Treaty of Cessions, 8 Stat. 200 in 1863
Gadsen Purchase, 10 Stat. 1031 (Dec. 30, 1853)
Bureau Of Land Management
Article IV, Sec. 3, Cl. 2

Notice Of Intent To Patent Land

To Whom It May Concern take notice:
Constitutional Mandate, Article 1, Section 8, Clause 18, parameters the quantity and usage of the lands ceded from the State to the united States of America. Preamble of the united States of America secures blessings to the posterity, one which is the Pursuit of Happiness as in the ownership of land, which is a right. All land is acquired by the posterity if it is not being utilized by Constitutional Mandate.

I hereby give notice to all the world and everyone, that the description of the area of land of the following meets and bounds are hereby within this document claimed for Allodial Land Patent:

Section _____   Township _____
Range _____

Lot # _____Block _____in the tract
_____.

I am not a resident of, I do not reside, and this is not a property of the bankrupt corporate USA, Inc. My filing is done under the Common Law and presents a Clouded Title to any existing Lien or claim otherwise. Common Law has the highest holding at Law. All Land Patent Claims are less any and all current Mining Claims that comply with the Acts of Congress on Mining in the years 1866 and 1872. These descriptions accept all questionable Land Patents of the united States of America.

Dated this _____ day of _____ 200 _____A.D.

I have the honor of being _____Sovereign American
Sui Juris, Jus Sanguinis, Jure Coronea

Right thumb print as my Common Law Seal;

Deuteronomy 19:15 – "So at the mouth of 2 or more witnesses, so shall the matter be established".

1.) _____
2.) _____

U.S. vs. Butterworth 267 U.S. 387. 45 S.Ct. 338. 69 L.Ed. 672. - Create your own common law forms/document.

William Wallace

Recording Requested By and Return to:

Name: _____, # _____Judicial District

C/O _____

City/State _____U.S.A. (no zip code/zone)

Non-Domestic

· ·

Notice Of Intent To Preserve Mineral Interest

Notice of intent to preserve and interest in real property from extinguishment pursuant to Common Law and Land Patent applications.

Lien Claimant is _____and my heirs and assigns. My proper venue is noted at the top of this document. Interest and real property known by:

Township _____

Range _____

Section _____

All mineral rights, regardless of character, whether fugacious or nonfugacious, organic or inorganic, whether created by grant of reservation, regardless of form, whether fee or lesser interest, mineral, royalty or leasehold, absolute or fractional, corporeal or incorporeal, including express or implied appurtenant surface rights, owned or claimed to be owned by Lien Claimant under the Common Law in any real property situated in the _____County, State _____ U.S.A. (no zip code/zone), We have this Affidavit of Truth which is the highest standing and Clouds the Title and notes that any equity judge who goes against any of this conducts pound-breach and is fully liable along with other charges to be added. I have never signed off and therefore there is a broken chain of Title.

Signed: _____a Sovereign American

Right thumb print as my Common Law Seal.

Deuteronomy 19:15 "So at the mouth of 2 or more witnesses so shall the matter be established".

1.) _____
2.) _____

NOTICE TO ALL BUYER BEWARE

Notice informing all potential buyers that any sale of property by the Sheriff _____ of _____ County is illegal and unlawful. The Sheriff is abusing his office and comes under Color of Law. The Sheriff is promoting fraud, deceit and corruption and passing along insolvency to all involved. The Sheriff commits these acts outside the courthouse because he knowing is violating the law.

I, _____, am a Sovereign American and have a Common Law Lien upon my property which cannot be removed or satisfied except by me. I have not and will not sign off the property. Therefore the Title is Clouded and there exist a broken chain of Title. Anyone found on my property is considered a trespasser. I am not responsible for the safety of anyone caught trespassing. I have the right and duty to defend my property including using deadly force. John Bad Elk v. U.S. I have established my Allodial Title and Land Patent to all conspirators trying to defraud the public by unlawful sale and felony theft. If necessary the Sheriff and his associates will be replaced and I shall have to perform his duties. The Posse Committals Act is in place.

The Sheriff, _____, has failed to fully disclose the truth and other officials such as Judges, auctioneer and Banks or Mortgage Co. being known as _____ and all other co-conspirators involved in this collusion shall be held accountable. There exist a Clouded Title in effect and force. To try to conduct any sale is to commit pound-breach and all violators shall be full liable as individuals. Hafer v. Melo, 502 U.S. 21 (1991). Their assault will institute distress and their signatures as well as their performance bond shall be lien, along with their real property, electronics, vehicles, holdings, hereditaments, savings etc. The Sheriff is responsible under the Andersons Rules for Sheriffs and by the U.S. Constitution. The Sheriff and all other commit treasonous acts and acts of genocide for which no amount of money can repair. This is an Affidavit of Truth and serves as an official Cease and Desist Order issued by me to halt any and all attempted sales and collections. There is no statue of limitations on fraud. It is a Class 4 Felony to promote a totalitarian government. You have the right to all paperwork and information. Any questions, consult the property owner.

You have been warned and Notice has been served. Date: _____

Property Owner:

_____, # _____Judicial District

C/O _____

City/State _____ U.S.A. (no zip code/zone)

Non-Domestic

When you file the description of your property with just your signature and don't use all rights reserved under the UCC, the county as holder in due course accepts it free of all claims, including yours. This means they can use your property for credit which is pledged for bonds to gain illegal credit to profit themselves. To have allodial title rights, you cannot have any contract with the government or anybody that takes away your rights. You cannot be a debtor, which means bankrupt. Land must be without leans and purchased with more than twenty dollars in gold or silver. There can be no address on the geographical description on the property. You need two or more witnesses, without a lawyer or notary public and you do not file the title with the government.

The individual, unlike the corporation, cannot be taxed for the mere presence of existing. The corporation is an artificial entity, which owes its existence and charter powers to the state; but, the individual's rights to live and own property are natural rights for the enjoyment of which an excise cannot be imposed. Redfield v. Fisher, 292 P. 813 (1930)

When you buy land, you hire an attorney, lawyer, who is an officer of the court. They file the deed as a tenure deed. This converts your right to own property to a privilege so that they can levy a tax.

Address is a place where mail or other communications will reach a person. Munson v. Bay State Dredging and Contracting Co. 314 Mass. 485, 50 NE 2d 633 636. Generally a place of business or residence; though it need not be. Black's Law, 6th Edition. Artificial persons do not have unalienable rights; they have only privileges granted by the government.

You have declared the property is own by an artificial person, a business with the same name as yours.

When you get a mortgage, your property is used as collateral. The banker cannot own property nor have any rights to an allodial title land, since they are giving credit for profit, which is unprotected by the Constitution. So to have the illusion of power for foreclosure, the agents right the title up using the phrase, "For one dollar and other valuable consideration…." They keep it under twenty dollars in gold or silver so they do not violate the 7th Amendment.

World Heritage Treaty UNESCO – All Land in America was traded away for debt – does not include Allodial Title

EMINENT DOMAIN CASES

Abraham Lincoln said, " Whoever deprives men or women of land and a home of their own upon the Earth not only dispossesses his fellow men of their rights, but flies in the face of God's law, and is defying him in puny, through merciless and wicked disobedience."

Applegate V. US, 25 F3d 1579 Fed. Cir. 1994
5th Amendment recognizes both federal government's rights to take private property for public use and property owner's right to just compensation.

Armor and Co. Inc. V. Inver Grove Heights, 2 F3d 276 8th Cir. 1993
Prohibition against taking private property for public use without just compensation may extend to regulation on property.

Eide V. Sarasota County, 908 F2d 716 11th Cir. 1990
Property owner can establish that zoning regulation has taken his or her property without just compensation in contravention of 5th Amendment by demonstrating that regulation goes too far that there is no provision to award him just compensation.

Fields V. Sarasota Manatee Airport Authority, 953 F2d 1299 11th Cir. 1992

Gully V. Southwestern Bell Telephone Co., 774 F2d 1287 5th Cir. 1985
Landowner and business man who loses as a result of eminent domain, both land upon which his business rests as well as business itself may be compensated both for market value of land and for profits he will not be able to recoup upon relocation and landowner who is compiled by eminent domain taking to redesign or restructure improvements already erected on taking land may have cost of redesign figured into valuation of land acquired by the taking.

Hall V. City of Santa Barbara, 833 F2d 1270 9th Cir. 1986
Right to occupy property is perpetually a type of interest that is protected by taking clause.

In Re Jones Truck Lines, Inc., 57 F3d 642 8th Cir. 1995
Purpose of taking clause is to bar government from forcing some people alone to bear public burdens that should be borne by public as whole.

Langenegger V. US, 756 F2d 1565 Fed. Cir. 1985
United States may be held responsible for taking even when its action is not the final direct cause of the property loss or damage.

Lucien V. Johnson, 61 F3d 573 7th Cir. 1995

When government takes property for public use it must pay interest, which is among other things, compensation for delay and getting money that is owed.

Parkridge Investors LTD V. Farmers Home Administration, 13 F3d 1192 8th Cir. 1994

Taking occurs when property owner suffers physical invasion of property and when government regulation denies all economically benefit or productive use of property.

Pennell V. City of San Jose, 485 US 1, 99 Led2d 1, 108 SCt 849 1988

Purpose of taking clause is to bar government from forcing some people alone to bear public burdens which, in all fairness and justice, should be borne by the public as a whole and just compensation for plaintiff in taking case is typically defined as fair market value of property on date it is appropriated.

Restigouche, Inc. V. Town of Jupiter, 59 F3d 1208 11th Cir. 1995

Types of constitutional challenges applicable to zoning decision are just compensation taking, due process taking, substantive due process and equal protection.

Shelden V. US, 7 F3d 1022 Fed. Cir. 1993

US V. Land, 62.50 Acres, 953 F2d 886 5th Cir. 1992

US V. Le Cooke Co. Inc., 991 F2d 336 6th Cir. 1993

Overcompensation for condemned property is as unjust to public as under compensation is to owner, and the landowner bears burden of probing value of land.

Wheeler V. City of pleasant Grove, 833 F2d 267 11th Cir. 1987

5th Amendment requires just compensation when United States takes private property, which generally means fair market value of property when appropriated.

Yuba Natural Resources Inc. V. US, 821 F2d 638 Fed. Cir. 1987

Fair market value of real property, what willing buyer would pay willing seller, is just compensation where land is condemned by the United States for all time, that is permanently.

Sources at the United States embassy in Beijing, China have confirmed at the United States of America has tendered to China a written agreement which grants to the People's Republic of China, an option to exercise Eminent Domain within the United States of America, as collateral for China's continued purchase of U.S. Treasury Notes and existing U.S. Currency reserves. The written agreement was brought to Beijing by Secretary of State Hillary Clinton. This means they can take the oil and natural gas fields and mines.

HERE COMES THE JURY

Article VI Sec. 2 – This Constitution, and the Laws of the United States which shall be made in Pursuance thereof; and all Treaties made, or which shall be made, under the Authority of the United States, shall be the supreme Law of the Land; and the Judges in every State shall be bound thereby, any Thing in the Constitution or Laws of any State to the Contrary notwithstanding.

Did you know that the jurors are judges of both facts and the Law? The Constitution was designed to hold the government in check.

The Judge should tell the jury of its rights to judge the Law as to the intent of the law makers, if it's a good or bad law, and the application to the case. The jury has the power to acquit even if it contradicts the Law.

The jury has the duty to judge the evidence and decide what facts are relevant to the case. As a juror you have the right to judge the Law and the facts, making you a judge.

The Judge is the umpire of the case. The juror judges the Law and facts using the US Constitutions' intent of the lawmakers and your moral conscience. The juror has the power to nullify any unconstitutional or unjust law. Under the Constitution if there is no injured party, there is no crime. Unless actually injured, the state cannot be the injured party.

Jury Nullification Rulings:

"Because of what appear to be Lawful commands on the surface, many citizens, because of their respect for what only appears to be law (Color of Law), are cunningly coerced into waiving their rights, due to ignorance." from the Supreme Court in U.S. v. Minker 350 U.S. 179 at 187; 76 S.Ct. 281 (1956).

"...there can be no doubt that the jury has an 'unreviewable and unreversible power...to acquit in disregard of the instructions on the law given by the trial judge....'" U.S. v Dougherty, 473 F.2d 1113, 1139 (1972). Other info related to Dougherty case: 16 Am Jur 2d, Sec. 177.

"In criminal cases juries remained the judges of both law and fact for approximately fifty years after the Revolution. However, the judges in America, just as in England after the Revolution of 1688, gradually asserted themselves increasingly through their instructions on the law. We recognize, as appellants urge, the undisputed power of the jury to acquit, even if its verdict is contrary to the law as given by the judge and contrary to the evidence. This is a power that must exist as long as we adhere to the general verdict in criminal cases, for the courts cannot search the minds of the jurors to find the basis on which they judge. If the jury feels that the law under which the defendant is accused is unjust, or the exigent circumstances justified the actions of the accused, or any reason which appeals to their logic or passion, the jury has the power to acquit, and the court must abide by the decision." U.S. v Moylan, 417 F.2d 1002, 1006 (1969)

"It may not be amiss, here, gentleman, to remind you of the good old rule, that on questions of fact, it is the province of the jury, on questions of law, it is the province of the court to decide. But, it must be observed that by the same law, which recognizes this reasonable distribution of jurisprudence, you have nevertheless a right to take it upon yourselves to judge of both, and to determine the Law as well as the fact in controversy...For, as on the one hand, it is presumed, that juries are the best judges of facts; it is, on the other hand, presumable, that the court are the best judges of law. But still, both objects are lawfully, within your power of decision." Justice John Jay to the jury, Georgia v. Brailsford, 3 Dall. 1, 4 (1794), 1 L.Ed. 483.

Sparf v. United States, 156 U.S. 51(1895) It may not be amiss here, gentlemen, to remind you of the good old rule that on questions of fact it is the province of the jury, on questions of law it is the province of the court, to decide. But it must be observed that, by the same law which recognizes this reasonable distribution of jurisdiction, you have, nevertheless, a right to take [156 U.S. 51, 65] upon yourselves to judge of both, and to determine the law as well as the fact in controversy. ...the jury has "...the power to bring in a verdict in the teeth of both law and facts." Oliver Wendell Holmes, Horning v D.C., 254 U.S. 135, 138, 41 S.Ct. 53, 54, 65 L.Ed. 185 (1920)

"...no fact tried by a jury shall be otherwise reexamined in any court of the United States, than according to the rules of the common law." U.S. Constitution, 7th Amendment. Only another common law jury can review a decision of a jury. There is no other appeal. Not even the Supreme Court can review a jury's decision.

A good juror must know the US Constitution. Without this knowledge you are vulnerable to power-hungry Judges and politicians. The jury is the protector of the people from the government. If the government dictates the standard of trial it dictates the results, making the judge a dictator.

Other Court Cases:
- Sei Fujii v. California – All judges are prejudice and bias. There are no fair trials. They are paid by IMF courts of equity.
- Atkins et al v. U.S. – Judges are members of an elite club.

"The jury has the right to determine both the Law and the facts." – Samuel Chase, U.S. Supreme Court Justice, 1796, and signer of the Declaration of Independence.

"Jurors should acquit, even against the judge's instructions...if exercising their judgment with discretion and honesty they have a clear conviction that the charge of the court is wrong." Alexander Hamilton, 1804.

"The jury has the power to bring a verdict in the truth of both law and face." – Oliver Wendell Holmes, U.S. Supreme Court Justice, 1902.

"I would remind you that extremism in the defense of liberty is no vice. And let me remind you also that moderation in pursuit of justice is no virtue." Barry Goldwater

"You can only protect your liberties in this world by protecting the other man's freedom. You can only be free if I am free." Clarence Darrow

CHALLENGING JURISDICTION

In the United States Constitution there are only two crimes, counterfeiting and treason. All other crimes are under state jurisdiction. This means all federal drug crimes are unconstitutional because they come under Title 2 U.S.C. and are not part of the Title 18 criminal code. The government is applying criminal sanctions to a civil law. Also, if your alleged drug crime occurred in only one state, it is illegal for the federal government to have jurisdiction. US vs. Scarborough, 431 US 563

A "Subpoena Duces Tecum" is a court summons ordering a named party to appear before the court and produce documents or other tangible evidence for use at a hearing or trial.

The summons is known by various names in different jurisdictions. The term "Subpoena Duces Tecum" appears to be used exclusively in the United States. It is a Latin phrase meaning "bring with you under penalty of punishment". The summons is called a "Subpoena for production of evidence" in some states that have sought to reduce the use of non-English words and phrases in court terminology.

The "Subpoena Duces Tecum" is similar to the subpoena ad testificandum, which is a writ summoning a witness to testify orally. However, unlike the latter summons, the Subpoena Duces Tecum instructs the witness to bring in hand books, papers, or evidence for the court. In most jurisdictions, a subpoena usually has to be served personally.

In the case of STATE OF IDAHO v. JOSEPH STEVENS CR-M97-76220. In this case a "Subpoena Duces Tecum" was filed with the court on February 23, 1998 asking questions about how jurisdiction was obtained. Assistant prosecutor Michael Maltby filed a Motion To Dismiss on February 27, 1998. The motion read impart "This motion is made on the grounds for the reason the State no longer wishes to proceed in this manner."

Why? Could it be that the government could not answer the Subpoena without exposing its fraud?

Look up status in your States Constitution. Example: Constitution of State of Georgia. Paragraph XXV - Status of the citizen. The social status of a citizen shall never be the subject of legislation. If it's not up to the legislation, then who is it up to? How about YOU?

The jails are full of criminals where there are no injured parties. This is a windfall for lawyers and Judges who get 10% to 25% of the fines for their retirement. It doesn't matter how crowded the jails are so long as the Judges get their money. This is a conflict of interest and could be considered a violation of the RICO [Racketeering] ACT.

If you have a problem with a Judge you can file a complaint with a sworn affidavit to the Judicial Qualification Commission in your state.

When you hire a lawyer you become wards of the court. The definition of wards of the court is infants or people of unsound minds; therefore, you can plead insanity because that was established when you hired the lawyer.

If you are forced to sign something that you don't want to sign, your signature is null and void if you put it in [brackets] or put TDC which stands for threat, duress or coercion by your name.

Other Court Cases: - Broom v. Douglas, 75 Ala. 268, 57 So 860 - U.S. v. Lopez

   — Sramek v. Sramek, 17 Kan. App. 2d 573, 576-77, 840 P.2d 553 (1992), rev. denied 252 Kan. 1093 (1993) - Melo v. U.S., 505 F.2d 1026

DON'T BE CRUDE

Oil comes from the mantle of the Earth, not from Dinosaurs. It is carbon produced with heat and pressure. It is a constant flow. It is always being capped off. This was discovered by the Russians in the 1940's. To get this technology Wall Street businessman Mikhail Khodorkovsky was ordered to acquire Yukos Oil Copmpany.

In Zapolyarmy, Russia the well Kola, SG – 3 is about 7 miles deep. As time goes by an oil well produces less because it is just getting clogged up. On land it is easier and less expensive, because you don't have to shut it down, to drill another oil well than to unclog. But, in the ocean it costs billions to set up an oil platform versus a couple of million to unclog it. There is an abundance of natural gas in America. You have to go through oil to get to natural gas. If the oil wells in America were re-opened America would not have to import oil. The oil companies create an artificial scarcity to legitimize price heights.

By creating a false shortage the OPEC monopoly can raise oil prices. Watch the 2006 Chris Paine movie, "Who Killed the Electric Car".

ULTRA DEEP OIL WELL DIAGRAM

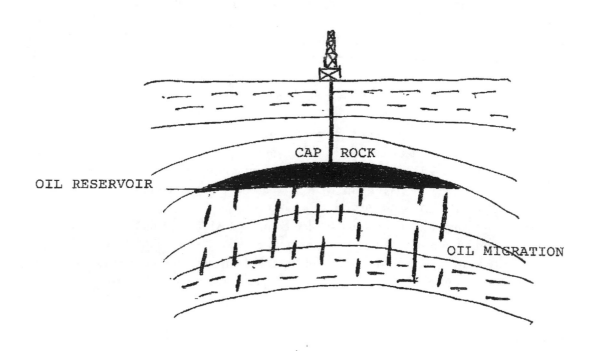

OIL COMPANIES CREATE AN ARTIFICIAL SCARCITY
TO LEGITIMIZE HIGH GAS PRICES

WACKO NOT OK

Waco – The jury found Waco survivors innocent but Judge Walter Smith reversed the juries decision and sentenced all the Davidians to a 40 year blanket sentence. The independent media is replacing mainstream media. The local stations and newspapers are simply taking any information put out by UPI and AP as the truth.

Oklahoma City – The unedited 4-K tape shows two bombs were removed from the building approximately 1 hour after the initial two blasts. There is no question that the building was blown from the inside concurrent with a car bomb outside which was confirmed by Mayor Ron Norick, local law enforcement and ATF. A car bomb with a twelve-hundred pound explosive pack was identified from the remains in the crater. Thirty six hours later brought the investigation to a Ryder truck. There were no remains found at the scene of the twenty-four foot Ryder truck. There was no fertilizer found at the scene. A rental agent at Elliott's Body Shop has a gag order against him. Retired Brigadier General Benton Parton says that even if it had been a ten-thousand pound fertilizer bomb it could not have blown up the concrete reinforced steel columns. The search warrant on Mr. McNichols farm was dated seven days before the bombing occurred. Seventeen ATF agents were absent from the building that day. One hundred sixty-eight non-government men, women, and children were murdered.

ENVIRONMENTAL UNPROTECTION AGENCY

The EPA was created through special interests. "Due process" means that we have some remedy in a court of law. But with the EPA we don't. The individual states will be far more effective handling their environmental problems on a state level. If you belong to an environmental Political Action Committee (PAC) please stop trying to buy politicians influence by throwing money at them. Instead take the money and buy tracks of land and set up species conservatories. The EPA takes away rights and bankrupts businesses and the people.

GET THE LEAD OUT

They show the commercial with the black lady living in a shack, watching her little baby eat paint chips. What kind of mother would watch her baby eat paint chips, leaded or unleaded?

It's okay to give your children all those vaccine inoculation shots even though their immune system is immature and the benefits are highly questionable. Children under fourteen are three times more likely to suffer adverse reaction after receiving hepatitis B shots than catch the disease. The state gets money from the drug companies for every child that is fully vaccinated.

You can put mercury and three-thousand other combinations of poison in your mouth; you can get tattoos with lead, mercury and anti-freeze. You can eat candies with lead from Mexico, but whatever you do, don't paint your house with lead paint. There are about twenty-four million homes with led paint. In some states, banks will not loan you money until you de-lead your house. Why, you ask? The government, like Superman, can't see through lead. Lead is the densest material on earth. Satellites can't spy on you to see what you are doing or how many guns you have or how much money you have. That is why there are those little strips in money. (When you drive by a policeman, they can detect how much money you have.) Lead paint has nothing to do with trying to protect your children. It's all about invasion of privacy.

Lead is in gasoline vapors, exhausts from cars, hair dyes, tobacco smoke, and used in soldering. It settles in the brain, nerves, bones, and in the right kidney. Fair skinned people take more lead in.

Have you ever seen a child eating paint chips? Why can't you use the existing paint as a primer and cover your walls with latex paint?

Home Remedies:

- Mix 6 oz. of Basil, 1 oz. each of Rosemary, Hyssop, and Boneset into a tea. Drink one cup, three times a day.
- Take one tablespoon of graded red cabbage 3 times a day.
- Cranberries.
- 2 tablespoons of ground pumpkin seeds, 1 tablespoon of powdered okra, and ½ teaspoon of cayenne pepper mixed in with 1 tablespoon of rhubarb sauce, three times a day for ten days.
- Sulfur baths; not oral.

ONE FLU OVER THE CUCKOO'S NEST

If you were born in the 1950s, you would have gotten 6 immune shots. Now you get 35. One of them is Chicken Pox which last 7 to 10 years. It is better to get the Chicken Pox as a child than as an adult, so you should avoid this shot. The drug companies pay the State money for everybody that gets their shots. One doctor wanted a release signed saying they would be responsible if the child had a bad reaction to the shot. They told the doctor that the child had to get the shot because the child might infect the other children. The doctor said that if the other children get their shots, how will my child infect them? His child did not have to get the shot. Another doctor said they don't know what will happen ten or twenty years down the road with these shots.

The following are inoculations which left undesirable residues: Tetanus causes constrictive nature, particularly in babies. Measles effect nerves in spine and trouble in spinal fluid and can cause MS. Mumps cause female cysts and often cause prostate trouble in later life. Measles and mumps residues can be carried over from childhood if these diseases are not carried for in a proper manner. The viruses can come out in the primes of people's lives. Black widows and brown spider bites effect nerves. Dog bites can cause convulsions, even many years later. Rattle snake bites cause constriction often in the throat producing constant cough or heart pain. It also can be in any animal product where the animal was bitten by a rattle snake.

In November of 2007, following the State of Maryland's threats against parents who refused to have their children vaccinated, children were herded into a Prince George County courthouse being guarded by armed personnel with attack dogs. Inside, the children were forcibly vaccinated, many against their will, under orders from the State Attorney General, various State Judges and the local School Board Director, all of whom illegally conspired to threaten parents with imprisonment if they did not submit their children to the vaccinations.

Home Remedies for Swine Flu: Before you get the flu, take 10-20 drops, depending on your weight, of pleurisy root in one once of water, in the AM and PM. If you have the flu, add natural vitamin C and colloidal silver. Selium supplements may be needed because acid rains has removed it from the soil.

Bacteria operates at a 100 Hz. Viruses used to operate at 1000 Hz, mutating in 200 days. Now they operate at 37,000 Hz, mutating every 28 days. When you have the flu, you have fever symptoms and your blood pressure is different on one side than the other. This is because the virus is not you, it is a foreign object.

Place an unpeeled onion in a dish in the rooms of your house. The onion will absorb bacteria. You can also cut both ends off an onion, put one end on a fork, and then place the fork end into an empty jar, placing the jar next to the sick patient at night. The onion will be black in the morning from germs. Placing onions and garlic around the room saved many from the black plague years ago. Garlic – capable of killing 23 kinds of bacteria including 60 types of fungi, yeast, and salmonella. Garlic also inhibits cancer in all tissues. Other Home Remedies:

- Elderberry juice
- Cayenne pepper
- Grapefruit
- Sip on red onion soup if you feel the flu coming

HOW THE GOVERNMENT MADE HIPPIES

In the mid 1950's, thousands of rhesus apes were imported to the United States. Their kidneys were injected with the polio virus. On the edge of death they were killed and the puss was extracted and put into fertile eggs. This created the Salk vaccine which was injected into children.

The polio puss was dead but a virus known only to be present in apes had slipped through. It was called Simian 40, or for short Sim 40 or SV 40. This virus is harmless to apes but when injected into the bloodstream of children, it created behavioral problems such as anguish, chills, depression, failing physical and mental health, fear, hatred toward the establishment, parents and teachers, laziness, listlessness, meningitis, suicide, and much more.

Physicians soon realized something went wrong with the injections. Big business propaganda hushed up the parents. Sterile water was injected temporarily, until they could figure out what was going on. A helper was bitten by an ape and he developed a fever. He developed the same symptoms as the children. Many of the children's immune systems were able to throw it off, but many were not. No one knew why these children were acting weird. The parents kicked them out of the house because it was embarrassing to take them out in public.

The Jewish race was the hardest hit. Out in the streets they found others who had the same problems. Because of the fear to be alone, nightmares, and coldness, they would sleep together. Marijuana was the only thing that helped. But the government made that illegal, saying that black men raped white women when they smoked it. Where were Jesse Jackson and Al Sharpton when you needed them the most?

Many have been institutionalized. Many have committed suicide. Many people, including children, have the virus in their system. It is in the spinal fluid and nervous system, which makes a RNA/DNA virus. It causes tension in the back of the neck and between the shoulder blades. Because it can stay dormant for many years and become active when you are weak, it is the most feared virus. Because of the virus, the US went from one of the most healthiest nations to one of the most sickest. To combat this, grind up one half a pound each of basil, kelp, and milk sugar. Take one teaspoon four times daily and water for six weeks. Because it is hidden, it may come and go for awhile, so keep on taking the herbal mixture. You will see the change to better health.

Dr. Eric Delwart is the researcher who, along with colleagues, made the discovery of contamination in Rotarix (a common children's vaccine). Using new technology to test eight infectious attenuated viral vaccines, the results shoed three of the vaccines contained "unexpected viral sequences":

1. A measles vaccine was found to contain low levels of the retrovirus avian leucosis virus
2. Rotateq, Merck's rotavirus vaccine, was found to contain a virus similar to simian (monkey) retrovirus
3. Rotarix (GlaxoSmithKine's rotavirus vaccine) was found to contain "significant levels" of porcine cirovirus 1. In their tests nearly 40 percent of the vaccines they tested contained viral contaminants. In lab tests, the virus was found to cause several different types of cancer, including brain cancer, and now SV40 is showing up in a variety of human cancers such as lung, brain, bone, and lymphatic.

A BOOBY PRIZE

The reason breast cancer is on a rise is because every time you get a mammogram you increase your chances of getting breast cancer by 2%. Mammograms at any age are not fool proof. Mammograms are usually more difficult to read in women before they hit menopause. The main draw back of mammography is that it's hard to differ between normal, dense tissue and cancerous tissue when looking for small tumors surrounded by glandular tissue. Because mammograms are more difficult to read in younger women, they have a high incidence of false positives and undergo more unnecessary biopsies.

Breast Cancer Awareness month is sponsored by pharmaceutical companies. Like AstraZeneca which manufactures the controversial breast cancer drug Tamoxifen™. This drug brings in hundreds of millions of dollars a year and is suspected to cause, among others, endometrial cancer. They also manufacture Acetochlor™ which almost certainly causes breast cancer and other herbicide-fungicides.

Taking pregnant mare's urine (PMU) and an estrogen pill for menopause and osteoporosis over a period of years increases your risk of breast cancer by 30-50% and endometrial cancer 6-8 times.

The way they get the PMU is they put a pregnant Mare in a small stall so that it doesn't move around. It has to stand up 24/7. The Mare is fed little water so that the urine will be more potent. When the horse is born, they slaughter the fold and the horse is impregnated again. This goes on for about fifteen years. Where is the Humane Society? I would rather be a Michael Vick's dog, than one of these horses. They also put horse urine in birth control pills. Birth control pills change personalities.

The alternative would be a thermogram. Thermography of the breast can detect abnormality 8-10 years before a mammogram. It does not harm the body and it is even safe for pregnant women. It is not expensive or painful. You only need one, where as with a mammogram, it seems they always have an excuse for you to do another one at your cost and pain. The reason thermograms are not used more today is the huge investment in mammography and the pharmaceutical corporations would lose billions.

People who have breast cancer have a lack of iodine. The higher the altitude, the more iodine the body requires. Kelp is iodine with traced minerals. Symptoms for deficiencies in iodine are: always feeling cold, dull listless appearance, dislike for moisture, dull pains under both shoulder blades, enlarged glands, goiter, headaches, heart and chest pressure, little interest in life, slow and dull mind, slow movements, puffy face and body, pulse alternating often, swelling of fingers, and swelling of toes.

You can make your breasts bigger by eating soy during puberty, it makes mountains out of molehills. Bras restrict growth so you should wear it loosely. About 70% of all women are wearing the wrong size bra. A tight bra cuts off circulation and if it has metal in it, it can cause cancer. To increase size you can jump on a trampoline by yourself (75% of trampoline injuries are with 2 or more people jumping at the same time) or ride a horse. Every girl at that age needs a horse.

Physicists have recently developed a new, painless ultrasound alternative to mammograms. Radiologists suspend a patients breast in water, and then send sound waves through the water using ultrasonic sensors to assemble a 3-D image of the breast that reveals cancer, larger than 5 millimeters in diameter. It is called computed ultrasound risk evaluation device or CURE. It does not use radiation, lasts one minute, and is completely pain-free. So far, it does in fact appear to be more accurate than mammography.

Children whose mothers breastfed them longer and did not mix in baby formula scored higher on intelligence tests. In many other countries, babies are breastfed for two years. Babies need mother's milk mentally and physically. All diseases are part mental. Babies are a miniature of the Earth. Everything is connected on a universal energy scale level. No other species would ever think of not breastfeeding their offspring. Baby formula is trying to fool Mother Nature and everybody knows it's not nice to fool Mother Nature.

Home Remedies to increase mothers milk

Alfalfa with blessed thistle.

One teaspoon of caraway seeds in eight ounces of cold water. Boil and simmer for a few minutes. Drink several cups a day.

Fennel seed in barley water.

Home Remedies for Sore Breasts

Grate raw carrots, and apply it to harden and sore breasts.

Bag balm is good for lumps or pain. You can get it at veterinarian supply stores.

For knots in breasts, grate raw carrots, make it into a poultice and put it over you breast. Simmer laurel leaves in oil and apply to breasts gently without pressure.

To pull out a tumor, take a tomato and remove the core. Make a poultice and apply it to the tumor. Change it every 6 hours for 72 hours.

For pain in left breast, make myrtle tea.

UNHEALTHY CARES

We cannot have a national healthcare. It is not a right or a privilege, it is unconstitutional. The US Supreme Court has repeated ruled that healthcare is beyond the power of the federal government. Healthcare is regulated to the States or the people under the 10th Amendment. Doctors can file 10th Amendment court challenges against any national healthcare program. With a monopoly on healthcare, you can raise the rates which means less money for you. Before insurance companies, healthcare was not that expensive. Americans are not being told the truth.

Luke 12:1 – In the mean time, when there were gathered together an innumerable multitude of people, insomuch that they trode one upon another, he began to say unto his disciples first of all, Beware ye of the leaven of the Pharisees, which is hypocrisy.

Luke 12:2 – For there is nothing covered, that shall not be revealed; neither hid, that shall not be known.

Luke 12:3 – Therefore, whatsoever ye have spoken in darkness shall be heard in the light; and that which ye have spoken in the ear in closets shall be proclaimed upon the housetops.

The spirit world knows everything. Nobody gets away with anything. All karma must be balanced out. Do unto others as you would have them do unto you because you are doing it to yourself.

HIPPOCRITICAL OATH

Hippocrates (460-377 BC) said, "Let food be your medicine and your medicine be your food."

I swear by Apollo Physician, by Ascelpius, by Hygeia, by Panacea and by all the gods and goddesses, making them my witnesses, that I will carry out, according to my ability and judgment, this oath and this indenture. To hold my teachers in this art equal to my own, and to my own parents; to make them my partners in my livelihood; when they are in need of money to share mine with them; to consider their families as my own, and to teach them this art, if they want to learn it, without fee or indenture; to impart precept, oral instruction, and all other instruction to my own sons and daughters, the sons and daughters of my teachers, and to indentured pupils who have taken the physician's oath. I will use treatment to help wrongdoing. I will keep pure and holy both my life and my art. I will not use the knife, not even on sufferers from stone, but I will give place to those who are craftsmen of that skill. Into whatsoever houses I enter, I will enter to help the sick, and I will abstain from all intentional wrongdoing and harm, especially from abusing the bodies of men or women, be they slave or free.

And whatsoever I shall see or hear in the course of my profession, as well as outside my profession, in my commerce with men or women, if it be what should not be published abroad, I will never divulge, holding such things to be holy secrets.

Now if I carry out this oath, and break it not, may I gain forever reputation among all men and women for my life and for my art; but if I transgress it and forswear myself, may the opposite befall me.

Dr. Hulda Clark, who wrote the books "The Cure for all Cancers," "The Cure for Advanced Cancers," "Syncrometer Science Laboratory Manual," "The Prevention of all Cancers," "The Cure for all Diseases," and "The Cure for HIV," has a clinic in Tijuana, Mexico called Century Nutrition. She treats mostly terminal cancer, AIDS patients, and undiagnosed cases. She has a 95% success rate. Her 5% failure rate is due to clinical emergencies that beset the advanced cancer sufferer. She says that all cancer patients have isopropyl alcohol and the intestinal fluke in their livers. The isopropyl alcohol is responsible for getting the fluke established. This can be cured with black walnut hull tincture and wormwood, which kills the adult flukes, and cloves, which kills the eggs. She would make a great Surgeon General, which the natural medicine people would rejoice to after they woke up from fainting, but has to operate in Mexico because her methods are not approved by the AMA. The pharmaceutical companies can't make any money with this formula. Doctors get kickbacks from the pharmaceutical companies for the prescriptions they write and chemotherapy.

In 1931 Dr. Otto Warburg won the Nobel Peace Prize in medicine for his discovery that cancer occurs in the absence of free oxygen. When the body becomes acidic, which is a PH under 7.0, oxygen is driven out of the body causing cancer and over 160 other diseases. Why are we searching for the cure for cancer when we gave an award for finding it?

Oxygen oil is made with extra virgin olive oil, grape seed oil and jojoba oil, ozonated with pure oxygen using no chemicals or preservatives. Tested in 1955 at Texas A & M University, it oxidizes lactic acid and toxins. [C10H1803] It is an effective treatment for aches, acne, age spots, bacterial infections, bed sores, bee stings, burns, fungus, germs, hemorrhoids, inflammation, insect bites, joint pains, lymphatic system, melanoma, muscle pains, prevents infection in after surgery wounds, psoriasis, ringworm, sweat gland infections, viruses and yeast infections. It rejuvenates skin cells by keeping them moisturized and detoxified. Rub 5 to 10 drops in problem area until absorbed.

To purchase a 2 oz. bottle of oxygen oil, mail a check or money order for $30.00 for one and $28.00 each for two or more to the following address. The price includes shipping and handling. Allow approximately one to two weeks for delivery.

Amjad Fatemi
930 Richmond Hill Drive
Marietta, GA 30068

Kidneys are the body's filters. One kidney filters the bottom half, one filters the top half. They have two different functions. One removes poisons, one removes parasites. Men suffer a great deal more from the right kidney, and women suffer a great deal more from the left kidney. The right kidney filters inorganic materials such as arsenic, copper, DDT, lead, and mercury. When overworked the kidney area becomes cold. The left kidney is sensitive to infections. With this problem, you should eliminate salt for a while. You may gradually add no more than 5 grams of sea salt. With kidney problems the forbidden foods are alcohol, already made convenience foods, brain, fish, liver, pork, red meat, and smoked meats. Home remedies for the right kidney are male fern tea, pumpkin seed tea, shaved grass tea, and watermelon seed tea. For the left kidney: corn silk, female fern, uva ursi, and watermelon. Kidney troubles are expressed in sore knees and finally swollen ankles. Two thirds of all people committed to mental institutions have kidney disorders.

Sodium Fluoride is added to city water and is only surpassed by cyanide and mercury in toxicity. It is contained in toothpaste, which is a by-product of the aluminum industry. Because it is inexpensive, the pharmaceutical companies used it instead of other more expensive, less harmful forms of fluoride. When you brush your teeth, your immune system, parotid, parathyroid, thyroid and thymus glands are shut down for at least 12 hours; 24 hours if you brush twice a day. It accumulates in the right kidney with other metals, causing kidney problems. You should brush your teeth with sea salt. The worst appliance in your house is the electric toothbrush. Your teeth may be clean, but the vibrations do terrible damage to your organs. It is especially damaging to children, who are still growing.

Tap water absorbs metal poisons from pipes and lead joints. It is important to run the water a few minutes to get this water safe, but the water is still filled with some harmful chemicals. If you pour the water from one container to another while blessing the liquid, this will oxygenate and energize it. Be careful when breathing steam from tap water, because of the chemicals added to it.

Chlorine is universally used to control bacteria in water and chemically bonds with the proteins in our body, causing dry skin and hair, eye irritation/redness and other health concerns. Chlorine is not only absorbed through the skin but vaporizes in the shower and is inhaled directly into the lungs.

Aluminum builds up in the neural tissue, especially in the brain, causing Alzheimer's. It causes pain in the spleen, kidney problems, and causes children to cry a lot. It is in cooking wear, it seeps through the coating of canned beverages, it's also in deodorant, anti-acids, baking powder, toothpaste, gasoline pumps, and gasoline vapors. Fair skin people take in more aluminum.
Home Remedy: Cayenne pepper, dulse, pumpkin seeds, okra, red cabbage, rhubarb root.

Arsenic is found in cigarette smoke, dental compounds, and pesticides. It causes leukemia and Alzheimer's(also caused by mold). It settles in brain and in muscles. Symptoms would be a constant backache, causing chiropractor adjustments not to hold, difficulty swallowing, burning pains in esophagus, stomach, sometimes bowel, loss of hair, brittle nails, nervousness, weakness, and anorexia.
Home Remedies:
- Cayenne pepper, dulse, pumpkin seeds, okra, red cabbage, rhubarb root.
- 1 tablespoon of raw Mexican sugar, three times a day.
- Sulfur baths; not oral.

Cadmium is a poison in process grains, dairy products, meats, fish, fertilizers, exhausts from cars, cigarettes, batteries, dentures, and soldering. It prevents the absorption of other minerals and settles in the heart and right kidney.
Home Remedies: Zinc, Paprika, or Cabbages.

Cigarette Smokers who for every pack they smoke are equal to one chest x-ray.
Home Remedies:
- Calamus Root.
- Apples.

Dioxin also known as Agent Orange is used in paper manufacturing. It is found in corn, and used in lawns and gardens. It settles in the brain, digestive system, and kidneys, and attracts viruses.
Home Remedy: 15 yellow mustard seeds per day.

Formaldehyde is in cheese, milk, and grains. If diet sodas get hotter than 80°, it turns into formaldehyde. This means you should get a discount on embalming fluid when you die.
Home Remedy: Take 200 mg of natural Vitamin C, 100 mg of B-15, and 1 teaspoon of baking soda, together twice a day for two weeks.

Mercury settles in the brain, nerves, and kidneys. It causes deafness, depression, irregular heartbeat, loss of vision, in coordination, numbness, sore mouth and gums, tremors, and kidney mal function. It is in pesticides, cosmetics, dental amalgam fillings, anti-fungus sprays, and batteries, which decompose in land fields and drain into ground water. Orientals take in more Mercury.

Home Remedies:
- Cayenne pepper, dulse, pumpkin seeds, okra, red cabbage, rhubarb root.
- Selenium.
- Sulfur baths; not oral.

Nickel is needed to hold tumors together. It causes epilepsy and can paralyze the spinal column. It is in hydrogenated oils and fats.

Home Remedy: Poppy seeds.

Nitrates are found in meats, the air, and foods around a heavy industry. It accumulates in the heart.

Home Remedy: Marshmallow root.

Other Home Remedies:
- Anti-biotic – Avocado seeds made into a tea.
- Antiseptic – Lemon juice externally on sores, corns, and gargle with it. Drink it with fevers.
- Anti-tumor – Garlic.
- Appetite loss in children – Cranberry juice or sauce.
- Arthritis –
  - One tablespoon of Epsom salt in warm water and soak for 20 minutes.
  - Flax seed oil externally or internally.
  - 2 teaspoons of apple cider vinegar, 2 teaspoons of honey, in 8 ounces of water, three times daily with meals.
  - Swiss chard
  - 1 tablespoon of whey and 1 of lecithin in juice twice a day
- Asthma –
  - Soak 2 pieces of cloth in apple cider vinegar and wrap around each wrist, secured with plastic wrap.
  - 1 tablespoon of wild plum tree bark syrup four times a day.
  - Cinnamon – 1 teaspoon of graded black radish with honey before bed.
  - 2 tablespoons of lemon juice before each meal.
- Autism –
  - A hearing problem in the womb, caused by high frequencies from too many sonograms, blenders, coffee grinders, lawn mowers, etc…
  - Vitamin B6, calcium, chromium and magnesium, with the avoidance of sugar and food allergens.
  - Wear purple over the womb.
  - Scalp acupuncture.
  - Eat easily digestible foods.
  - Avoid cold drinks or food.
  - Eat five small meals a day, using fruits, nuts and seeds for snacks.
  - Keep the environment and routine familiar.

- ◦ Dogs, cats, fish and birds can help in the healing process.
- ◦ Decorate with bright colors.
- ◦ Get plenty of sunshine.
- ◦ Listen to classical music every day.
- ◦ Optimistic parents give energy to the child.
- ◦ Do brain exercises.
- Bacterial infections –
  - ◦ Black pepper.
  - ◦ Cabbage.
  - ◦ Cinnamon.
  - ◦ Garlic.
  - ◦ Goldenseal root.
  - ◦ Onions.
  - ◦ Whole green foods.
- Bee sting –
  - ◦ In mouth or throat, take one teaspoon of salt in mouth immediately to prevent strangulation.
  - ◦ Rub on raw onion.
- Birthmarks – Apply castor oil for several months. Wounds from past lives.
- Blackheads –
  - ◦ Vitamin A
  - ◦ Cucumber peelings over blackheads
  - ◦ Rub fresh strawberries over your face
- Blood pressure –
  - ◦ High – Potassium from fruits and vegetables.
  - ◦ High and low – Garlic.
- Boils –
  - ◦ Flax seed poultice
  - ◦ Sage and corn meal poultice
- Brain food –
  - ◦ Coconut meat, and milk.
  - ◦ Boiled leaks in soups or salads.
- Burns –
  - ◦ Aloe Vera
  - ◦ Slightly beaten egg whites
  - ◦ Ice cold black tea poured over the burn repeatedly
- Cancer - Polyphenols from green tea stops cancer cells from growing. People who do not drink green tea once a day are five times more likely to get cancer whether they smoke or not.
- Chemotherapy –
  - ◦ Two lbs of baking soda, and two lbs or sea salt in a tub for 40 minutes neutralizes chemotherapy.
  - ◦ Golden Grain or Everclear, mix 50.50 with water. Use to sanitize areas like hands, vents, doorknobs, and inside soles of shoes.
- Chicken soup – Neutralize hormones and toxins of meats by rubbing it with sea salt and let it sit for an hour. Rinse for fowl. You can also use buttermilk. This will improve digestion, reduce allergies, gives relaxation and strength.

- Children who are misbehaving – Cranberry juice with cloves, cinnamon, and honey.
- Children who do not talk – Fresh strawberries.
- Cholesterol – removes plaque.
  ○ Cranberry sauce or one cup of juice per day.
  ○ Alfalfa sprouts.
- Chromium Poison – Thyme tea.
- Claustrophobia – green apples
- Cuts –
  ○ honey as an antiseptic.
  ○ pepper stops pain with pressure
- Depression – There are 7 different degrees of depression therefore there should be 7 different cures. Prozac – releases depression on right side of brain which makes left side hyperactive and can make a person go crazy as in Columbine.
- Diabetes – a liver stress issue.
  ○ 100 gm of wheat flower, 100 gm of gum (of tree) (gondh), 100 gm of barley, and 100 gm of black seeds (kalunji), in five cups of water. Boil for 10 minutes and allow it to cool down by itself. When it becomes cold, filter out the seeds and put in glass container. Take one small cup of this mixture in the morning on an empty stomach for 7 days. The next week, take it every other day.
  ○ Cinnamon.
  ○ 2 cups of dwarf leaf tea per day.
  ○ White fig compress over throat.
  ○ Garlic.
- Drug residue – Lima beans, bell peppers, and sweat potatoes, once a day for seven days.
- Earache – Tape garlic clove in ear.
- Energy –
  ○ 1 cup of alfalfa sprouts, 10 almonds, 3 cups of pineapple juice, and 1 cup of water.
  ○ Blackstrap molasses.
  ○ Grapes.
  ○ ½ tablespoon of flax seed, steeped in ½ pint of hot water, twice per day.
  ○ 2 tablespoons of dates and sunflower seeds blended with 8 ounces of water.
  ○ 1 quarter teaspoon of sea salt, 1 lemon, and 6 ounces of water. Sip for two hours.
- Enzyme supplier – Pineapple.
- Feeling cold – Seaweed, kelp, and cayenne pepper, in hot water.
- Feeling hot – Motherwort.
- Female bleeding – 2 tablespoons of cooked okra three times a day.
- Fever –
  ○ Drink liquids only. Diluted apple or grape juice, cherry juice, lemonade, limeade, orange juice, and herbal tea with honey. Fasting for a period of two days.
  ○ Pleurisy root
  ○ Chaparral three times a day for one month for tic fever
  ○ Hot lemon juice with honey
- Food poisoning –
  ○ Ginger tea with honey
  ○ Nutmeg
  ○ Gentian
  ○ Charcoal tablets

- ◦ 2 teaspoons of apple cider vinegar with honey in 7 ounces of warm water. Sip slowly.
- Hearing loss –
  - ◦ Manganese
  - ◦ Marigold
  - ◦ Zinc
- Insect bites –
  - ◦ Rub sage tea on area.
  - ◦ Plantain leaf.
  - ◦ Yellow Onion.
  - ◦ Raw apple on bite.
- Insect Repellant – Rub parsley tea on skin.
- Insulin producer – Cucumber.
- Kidney Infection – Only watermelon for two days.
- Kidney Inflammation –
  - ◦ Only watermelon and its seeds for two days.
  - ◦ One radish three times a day.
- Kidney and bladder problems –
  - ◦ Celery tops for five weeks after each meal.
  - ◦ 7 oz of half cranberry juice/half water three times a day.
- Laryngitis – Black beans.
- Leukemia –
  - ◦ Grape seed extract – stimulates leukemia cells to commit suicide within 24 hours. 76% of leukemia cells exposed to the extract were killed off while healthy cells were unharmed.
  - ◦ Okra.
  - ◦ Red beats.
  - ◦ Zinc.
- Liver flukes – 10 drops of Clorox in 8 ounces of water – it also kills whatever else is in the stomach.
- Liver food –
  - ◦ Dandelion leaves.
  - ◦ Sweetish bitters – opens up the liver and good especially for cancer. 1 tablespoon per month in 8 ounces of water.
- Memory –
  - ◦ Basil.
  - ◦ Coconut meat.
  - ◦ Cardamom.
  - ◦ 6 to 10 almonds per day or 1 teaspoon of almond oil.
  - ◦ Sage.
  - ◦ 4 cloves in tea daily.
  - ◦ 2 mustard seeds daily.
  - ◦ 3 prunes daily.
  - ◦ Vitamin B12.
  - ◦ Folic acid.
  - ◦ Gotu Kola.
  - ◦ Rosemary tea in the morning.
  - ◦ Alfalfa seeds and dill seeds for children.

- Ginko.
- Kava kava.
- Metal poisoning –
  - Green beans and Zucchini only for 3 days.
  - Squash and strawberries.
- Mineral supplier – Alfalfa seeds.
- Moody – Fish oil.
- Morning sickness –
  - Peach leaf tea.
  - Ladies mantle – curbs appetite.
  - Peppermint chamomile – feeling of satisfaction.
  - Cayenne pepper or hawthorn tea – circulation.
  - Kelp and dulse for seasoning food – thyroid.
  - Parsley – kidneys.
  - Cottage cheese with paprika – glands.
- Mosquito bites – Soap.
- Mouth odor –
  - Caraway seeds
  - Juniper berries
  - Parsley
- Multiple Sclerosis (MS) – Avocado and Pineapple
- Muscle builders –
  - Beans and corn
  - Rye
- Muscle pain – Rub raw potato over the muscle
- Muscle strengthener – Buckwheat
- Osteoporosis – Agave
- Pinkeye – Red potatoes over eye
- Pituitary – Cherry juice
- Pleurisy – Flax seed tea
- PMS –
  - Thyme
  - Yams
  - Okra – heavy bleeding
  - Sage
  - ½ cup of cramp bark tea twice a day – for cramping
  - Apply ice to the nipples to stop uterine bleeding
  - Oats – for estrogen deficiency
- Pneumonia – Cranberry juice
- Poison Ivy – Epsom salt
- Poisons – Swallow charcoal tablets or burnt toast
- Pregnancy –
  - Between the second and fifth month, the unborn child needs 150 additional calories and from the sixth to the ninth month, the unborn child needs 300-400 calories over the need of the mother. The unborn child needs minerals; it needs calcium, iron, magnesium, zinc, and trace minerals. The fetus needs 34 grams of pure calcium to develop properly and if needed, will take it from the mother. When in pregnancy,

a mother should have a low salt diet. She can have all the fluid she wants without causing edema. The normal development of a child is dependant on enough vitamins A (carrots), B-Complex, C-Complex, D, and E. (100 units is needed for the baby).

- ◦ Coconut milk on empty stomach in the morning
- ◦ Peaches
- Prostate – Coconut milk
- Protein –
  - ◦ Avocado
  - ◦ Lentils
  - ◦ Meat
  - ◦ Millet
- Radiation –
  - ◦ Miso soup
  - ◦ Seaweed
  - ◦ ½ lb of salt and 1 lb of baking soda added to your bath
- Radioactive fallout – ¼ teaspoon of cinnamon, ¼ teaspoon of tartar, and ¼ teaspoon of powdered clove in 8 ounces of cranberry juice
- Rejection of offspring – Manganese - Symptoms: bones crackling when walking, burning sensation in body and limbs, crying spells, disliking children, enlarging of ovaries, eyes are red and swollen, fainting spells, glands are swollen, mentally disagrees with everything, murder of children, tender nipples, wanting to be left alone, womb falling and protruding.
- Stop smoking –
  - ◦ Chew or cook calamus root in apple juice
  - ◦ Laurel leaves
- Strep – Cucumber juice 5 times a day
- Stroke –
  - ◦ Shave head and apply tofu compress to be changed when tofu gets yellow
  - ◦ Wash limps with tobacco water if paralyzed
  - ◦ Rosemary for prevention
- Suicidal – 2 cups or more of black tea with honey
- Swelling –
  - ◦ Ankles – Adzuki beans, as a soup, or drink the fluid twice a day
  - ◦ Knees – Raw white cabbage poultice
- Tonsils –
  - ◦ Baked banana compress with olive oil
  - ◦ Grapefruit juice
- Toothache –
  - ◦ Black tea bag in hot water, then apply to cheek
  - ◦ Hyssop between tooth and gum overnight
  - ◦ Oil of clove on tooth
  - ◦ Pepper and mustard in a cloth over cheek
  - ◦ Powdered milk on tooth
- Tumors – 2 tablespoons morning and night of blended canned asparagus
- Weight reducing –
  - ◦ Leeks
  - ◦ Fresh carrot juice, can add fresh apple juice for better taste (Not store bought)

Proper Food Combining:

Green vegetables taking 5 hours to digest and to be eaten with acidic fruit, all protein, and all starch: Bamboo Shoots, Cabbage, Cucumber, Celery, Dandelion, Garlic, Lettuce, Onions, Peppers, Radish, Rhubarb, Spinach, Sprouts, and Watercress.

Mild starch taking 5 hours to digest and to be eaten with fat, green vegetables, and starch: Artichoke, Asparagus, Beats, Broccoli, Carrots, Cauliflower, Eggplant, Green Beans, Leeks, Rutabaga, Turnips, Okra, and Zucchini.

Starch taking 5 hours to digest and to be eaten with fat, green vegetables, and mild starch: Bread, Cereal, Chestnuts, Corn, Crackers, Grains, Lima Beans, Pasta, Peanuts (raw), Potatoes, Pumpkin, Squash, and Yams.

Protein fat taking 12 hours to digest and to be eaten with acid fruit, fat, and green vegetables: Avocado, Nuts (raw), Olives, and Seeds.

Protein (meat) taking 12 hours to digest and to be eaten with green vegetables: Beef, Chicken, Duck, Eggs, Fish, Goose, Pork, Rabbit, Seafood, Turkey, Veal, and Lamb.

Fat taking 12 hours to digest and to be eaten with all starches, green vegetables, and protein fat: Butter, Cream, Margarine, and Oil.

Acid fruits taking 2 hours to digest and to be eaten with green vegetables and protein fat: Acerola Cherries, Cranberries, Currents, Gooseberries, Grapefruit, Grapes (sour), Kumquat, Lemons, Limes, Oranges, Peaches (sour), Pineapple, Plums (sour), Pomegranate, Strawberries, Tangelo, Tangerine, Tomatoes.

Melon fruit taking 2 hours to digest and should be eaten alone: Cantaloupe, Honeydew, Muskmelon, Nutmeg, Papaya, and Watermelon.

Sub-acid fruit taking 2 hours to digest and should be eaten alone: Apricots, Blackberries, Boysenberries, Cherries (sweet), Elderberries, Figs, Eggplant, Guava, Huckleberries, Kiwi, Nectarine, Peaches, Plums, Prickly Pears, and Raspberries.

Dried, sweet fruit taking 3 hours to digest and should be eaten alone: Apricots, Bananas, Dates, Figs, Peaches, Pears, Pineapples, Prunes, and Raisons.

Dairy taking 12 hours to digest and should be eaten alone.

Apples taking 2 hours to digest and Rice taking 5 hours to digest can be combined with anything.

- Eat proteins and carbohydrates at separate meals.
- Eat only one concentrated protein at each meal.
- Fruit and vegetable juices as whole foods.
- Take milk alone.
- Cold foods including liquids inhibit digestion.
- Only eat fruit alone as a fruit meal.
- Fruits should not be eaten between meals while other food is digesting in the stomach.
- Do not eat sweet fruits and acid fruits together.
- Melons are best eaten alone but can be mixed with acid and sub-acid fruits.

Your health is your wealth.

ELECTRA FRIED

Electrical influence causes an alkaline body to go acidic, causing inflammation which blocks wellness, and scars the cell walls preventing hydration which is needed for the repairing of cells.

Electricity is built up in a body over a period of time. This results in the short circuiting of the electric body. This is being mislabeled as an immune system disorder. Some of the symptoms are anxiety, depression, mood swings, irregular heartbeat, fatigue, muscle aches, pain, colon problems, upset stomach, allergies, respiratory problems, discomfort near electrical devices, and sensitivity to light, noises, smell, and taste.

Radioactive chemicals are released from nuclear power, weapons industry, and other industrial pollutions are called fallout. Radiation lingers in the grass that animals eat, air (especially after rain and snow), and water.

Home Remedies are:
- ¼ teaspoon of cinnamon, ¼ teaspoon of cream of tartar, ¼ teaspoon of powdered clove, in 8 ounces of cranberry juice.
- 1 cup of willow leaf tea.
- 1 teaspoon of baking soda, 1 teaspoon of sea salt, ½ teaspoon of cream of tartar in 1 quart of water; Drink 8 ounces every 2 hours.
- Charcoal removes fallout but you need to eat the acidophilus to restore the good bacteria. It is in yogurt. Charcoal tablets are also good for food poisoning.
- Vitamin A, B-Complex especially B – 15, and Vitamin C.
- Take Ginseng, Valerian Root, and Passa Flora.
- 1 pound each of baking soda and sea salt in your bath water, soak for 20 minutes.

A Home Remedy for X-Ray Radiation: Fill a paper sack, half with baking soda and the other half with sea salt. Rub the bag over the affected area for two minutes. Throw the bag away.

A Home Remedy for Radon Poisoning: 2 teaspoons of liquid chlorophyll in 6 ounces of water, taken with 500 milligrams of Vitamin C three times daily for one week. Vitamin C should be natural. Synthetic Vitamin C weakens arteries. This formula also removes carbon dioxide poisoning.

Smoke detectors should be photoelectric. Many contain americium, radium, and plutonium, which are radioactive.

Power lines should be as far away as possible from your living space. They cause spiritual and physical damage.

Microwaves ruin the vibration of food cooked in it. All family members are affected by the waves, but the men are most harmed, especially the younger boys, whose male organs are still growing. A boy who eats micro waved food, has constant problems, and will not develop properly and develop to his full potential. Throw your microwave away or give it to your worst enemy for Christmas. They will say, "I thought you hated me, and here you are giving me this nice microwave."

Electric clocks next to your bed damage your Aura. The worst are the ones with the red lights on them. You should sleep in total darkness. Night lights cause cancer in children.

Computers give off electromagnetic radiation. This is most damaging to females, especially if they are pregnant. To combat this, use a computer pillow either on your lap of behind your back.

Electric blankets put holes in our Aura, which causes physical and spiritual damage. It also damages our blood and lymph systems, which can worsen leukemia and cancer. It makes a great present for your enemies.

Waterbeds contain an electric heater, which causes the same problems as an electric blanket. Back problems may be relieved, but they are damaging to the spinal fluid.

NINE STAR KI

Ki energy is the energy that controls the universe. The message of the Ki given by the ancients is know your strengths and weaknesses and how to use them: knowing the right way to proceed can make life entirely different. There are 108 personalities. The reason is because it is a 9 year cycle changing every month. (9 x 12 = 108) It is also a 9 year cycle inside an 81 year cycle and a 120 year cycle divided into two 60 year cycles. You have three numbers which are the basic, control, and tendency numbers. The way you get your basic number is: keep adding all the numbers of the year of your birth until you get one number, and then subtract it from 11. Example: 1974 = 21 = 1 + 2 = 3 - 11 = 8. Each year begins on February 4th. This is the halfway point between the winter solstice and the spring equinox. If you were born between January 1 and February 3, your birth year is the previous year.

1 water gives energy to 3 and 4 tree
3 and 4 tree gives energy to 9 fire
9 fire gives energy to 2, 5, and 8 soil
2, 5, and 8 soil gives energy to 6 and 7 metal
6 and 7 metal gives energy to 1 water

The lower elements, which are more yin, of the same kind gives energy to the higher elements, which are more yang. Example: 3 gives energy to 4, 2 gives energy to 5 and 8, 5 gives energy to 8, 6 gives energy to 7. The same elements have a cooperating relationship. People don't see how a certain couple could be attracted to each other. No one knows the energy that one person gives to another and that energy changes every year.

1 water gives into 2, 5, and 8 soil
2, 5, and 8 soil gives into 3 and 4 tree
3 and 4 tree gives into 6 and 7 metal
6 and 7 metal gives into 9 fire
9 fire gives into 1 water

Doctors treat the symptoms, not the cause. You cure a Yin disease with Yang, and a Yang disease with Yin. The larger organ in each group is Yin, the smaller is Yang.

Cause:	Effect/Symptom:
Kidneys, Bladder	Heart, Small Intestine
Stomach, Pancreas, Spleen	Kidneys, Bladder
Liver, Gall Bladder	Stomach, Pancreas, Spleen
Lungs, Large Intestine	Liver, Gall Bladder
Heart, Small Intestine	Lungs, Large Intestine

Example: Pancreatic cancer is a liver disease because the pancreas gives into or is controlled by the liver. Note: Tonsils help the spleen and the appendix helps the immune system.

Foods that give energy:
Water – azuki beans, buckwheat, compact, spike greens, seaweed, and salty taste.
Soil – millet, round vegetables, and sweet taste.
Tree – barley, oaks, wheat, fast growing, young greens, sprouts, and sour taste.
Metal – brown rice, root vegetables, and pungent taste.
Fire – corn, large leafy greens, and bitter taste.

People who live in North America should eat foods grown within 250 miles in any direction of where you live. You need energy from around the area you live. You don't need the energy of where you are not going to be. If you are going on a trip, you should eat food that is in harmony with the environment of your destination. You should start 4 days before your trip.

You should eat organic food. However, unless you grow it yourself, you do not know what fertilizer was used. A lot of fertilizer has ammonia nitrate in it. This is the gas used to kill Jews. Hitler learned about it from Stalin in Communism 101. They were both Nutzis and their motto was 'The Fuhrer, the better.' Who was worse, the student or the teacher? When you buy vegetables in planters, you'll see little white specs in the dirt. These specs are Styrofoam, which is poisonous. I guess they have to get rid of it somehow, so why not put it in your garden?

We interrupt this book for a very important message from the President of Alcoholics Unanimous. When traveling over 250 miles:

Mr. President

- If you are going to the beach and want to get lucky, drink Sex on the Beach.
- If you are visiting the Queen, drink Crown Royal.˙
- If you are visiting your grandmother, drink Grand Marnier.˙
- If you are visiting your grandfather, drink Old Granddad.˙
- If you are visiting gay people, any cocktail will do.
- If you are visiting a spy, drink a martini shaken, not stirred.
- If you are going to Alaska, drink Yukon Jack.˙
- If you are going to New York, drink a Manhattan.
- If you are going hunting, drink Killer Kool-Aid.
- If you are going mining, drinking Goldschlager.˙
- If you are going to highjack a ship, drink Captain Morgan.˙
- If you are going to Tobacco Road, drink Moonshine.
- If you are going to Skid Row, drink MD 20/20.˙ Also good for dog bites.

I do not approve of drinking and driving. The deaths are down but the amounts of DUI's are the same. DUI's for women are up 30%. There are some women who can have one drink and be considered driving under the influence. This is money in the bank for lawyers and Judges. The easiest way to sober up is to eat honey. It removes alcohol from the blood extra fast. This does not mean you can sober up with Baron Yager.˙ The next best way is to eat cucumbers. It has an enzyme called erepsin which reduces the alcohols intoxicating effect. People who drink too much suffer from deficiencies of vitamins B - complex B1 B12 - C, and E, choline, inositol, niacin, pantothenic acid, and zinc. To reduce the desire for alcohol, mix chromium and vanadium. Take one teaspoon twice a day.

The 12 Zodiac signs, which are established because Jupiter, the largest planet in this universe, takes 12 years to circle the sun.

Rat, Rabbit, Horse, and Rooster will always be a 1, 4, or 7.
Ox, Dragon, Sheep, and Dog will always be a 3, 6, or 9.
Tiger, Snake, Monkey, and Boar will always be a 2, 5, or 8.

6 guidelines of to a relationship.

1 – basic number – attraction number – no one knows the energy that one person gives to another

2 – control number – people with the same control numbers can understand each other more clearly even if you don't like the person

3 – tendency number – people with the same tendency numbers have the same approach to life and may have the same habits

4 – whether the reciprocal relationships of the 5 elements are cooperating or conflicting

5 – family – you may be attracted to the energy that you are around growing up

6 – business is easier if the basic numbers are compatible and have good communication

Control numbers are a 3 year cycle: Date indicated is when month usually starts but on rare occasions, can start on the day before or the day after, except in February only on the day after.

Basic #	1, 4, 7	3, 6, 9	2, 5, 8
4 February	8	5	2
6 March	7	4	1
5 April	6	3	9
6 May	5	2	8
6 June	4	1	7
7 July	3	9	6
8 August	2	8	5
8 September	1	7	4
9 October	9	6	3
8 November	8	5	2
7 December	7	4	1
6 January	6	3	9

Tendency numbers are a 9 year cycle:

Basic #	9	8	7	6	5	4	3	2	1
4 February	9	2	4	6	8	1	3	5	7
6 March	1	3	5	7	9	2	4	6	8
5 April	2	4	6	8	1	3	5	7	9
6 May	3	5	7	9	2	4	6	8	1
6 June	4	6	8	1	3	5	7	9	2
7 July	5	7	9	2	4	6	8	1	3
8 August	6	8	1	3	5	7	9	2	4
8 September	7	9	2	4	6	8	1	3	5
9 October	8	1	3	5	7	9	2	4	6
8 November	9	2	4	6	8	1	3	5	7
7 December	1	3	5	7	9	2	4	6	8
6 January	2	4	6	8	1	3	5	7	9

Example: May 2, 1910 has a basic number of 9, a control number of 3 and a tendency number of 2.

During and after growth, the father influence the child's intellectual, social, and ideological character. The mother influences the child's physical, sensory, and emotional character. The child is a product of what the mother is doing during pregnancy. Emotions can be transferred from the mother in the womb. Everything physical started as emotional. You hold emotions in your organs. You cannot change your inherited character, but through food you can change the quality of your character. Eating the same foods with your family will put you in harmony and establish better communication. A family that eats together stays together. The person that prepares your food is putting their love and energy into the food. That is why when you leave home you may have withdrawals because you are missing your mother's cooking. When two people live together, eat the same foods, and exchange their chemical makeup through kissing, touching, and sex, their DNA changes taking on the characteristics of the other. So no matter what your birth sign is, once you have a partner you can change yourself enough to keep commitment through life.

More Yin   9   2   3   4   Less Yin

More Yang   1   8   7   6   5   Less Yang

Yin people do better in yin years and months. They like hot weather. Prefer sweets, salads, fruits, liquids, and vegetables. Function better with a new moon. Can't see the forest for the trees.

Yang people to better in yang years and months. They like cold weather. Prefer animal food, salty food, baked dishes, sea vegetables, drier foods, and more cooked foods. Function better with a full moon. Can't see the trees for the forest.

In a 5 year like 2004, everyone is in their own house meaning everyone will like to be with people with their own basic number. In 2005 it will be their basic number plus 1, in 2006 it will be their basic number plus 2, in 2007 it will be their basic number plus 3, and so on. Another way to say this is people will want to be with the following basic number when they will be the following ages from Feb. 4th to Feb 3rd of the following year:

You will be attracted to 5's at the age of: 18, 27, 36, 45, 54, 63, keep adding 9.
You will be attracted to 6's at the age of: 19, 28, 37, 46, 55, 64, keep adding 9.
You will be attracted to 7's at the age of: 20, 29, 38, 47, 56, 65, keep adding 9.
You will be attracted to 8's at the age of: 21, 30, 39, 48, 57, 66, keep adding 9.
You will be attracted to 9's at the age of: 22, 31, 40, 49, 58, 67, keep adding 9.
You will be attracted to 1's at the age of: 23, 32, 41, 50, 59, 68, keep adding 9.
You will be attracted to 2's at the age of: 24, 33, 42, 51, 60, 69, keep adding 9.
You will be attracted to 3's at the age of: 25, 34, 43, 52, 61, 70, keep adding 9.
You will be attracted to 4's at the age of: 26, 35, 44, 53, 62, 71, keep adding 9.

Your basic number kicks in at 18 because it takes you 18 years to grown into it, affecting your character and destiny. Until then, your personality is more your control number. After 18, your control number continues to influence your personality mainly in emotions and outward expressions. Opposites attract, meaning: 1's and 9's attract, 2's and 8's attract, 3's and 7's attract, and 4's and 6's attract. People who are born 6 months apart are attracted to each other. People who are born in opposite areas are attracted to each other. The influence of your birth order is important, too. Don't marry what you are. Example: If you are a first born, don't marry a first born. If there is a 5 year difference between ages of the last sibling born before you, you have first born tendencies. Usually, first born girls become nurses because they take care of the younger siblings.

To attract 1 water's, wear the color black. To attract 2, 5, and 8 soils', wear the color blue. To attract 3 and 4 tree's, wear the color red. To attract 6 and 7 metals, wear the color white. To attract 9 fire's, wear the color yellow.

5 Soil – up and down – When you are in the 5 house, you want to be with 5 soils. The earth's atmosphere is closely aligned to your energy. Everything naturally comes to you, both negative and positive. You should be cautious and avoid drastic changes. It is not the best time for starting a new business. You should be well organized. The first 6 months of the year usually go smoothly, while during the next 6 months the obstacles usually appear. Being patient and flexible can help you pass through hard times. You are more perceptible to blood diseases, bronchitis, colds, and traffic accidents. You will experience the positive and negative aspects of love. The negative approach will become more predominant if you act aggressively. You may meet someone from your past. You should eat more naturally sweet flavors like carrots, onions, and squash. You will be in the 5 house starting February 4 of the year you will be 18 + keep adding 9 years.

6 Metal – prosperity – When you are in the 6 house, you want to be with 6 metals. It's time to reap the rewards or your previous activities. Your finances may improve and your business is more successful. Don't be overconfident or dishonest. Don't exceed your capacity and manage your resources well. Be careful when borrowing or lending money. You may be prone to exhaustion, mental fatigue, heart trouble, insomnia, and accidents. You should rest, eat good food and chew it well, or you risk putting your health in danger, which could last for some time. Listening to and getting

advice from other people can make it a good year for developing yourself. You will be in the 6 house starting February 4 of the year you will be 19 + keep adding 9 years.

7 Metal – joy – When you are in the 7 house, you want to be with 7 metals. Your goals are accomplished and things go smoothly. You could receive good news and make new friends, improve finances and be satisfied mentally. It is better to stay with activities and patterns that have already been established. You may experience problems with your heart, kidneys liver, lungs, neurosis, and stress. You should take care of your teeth. Be careful with jealousy of the opposite sex. You will be in the 7 house starting February 4 of the year you will be 20 + keep adding 9 years.

8 Soil – change or revolution – When you are in the 8 house, you want to be with 8 soils. You may change where you live, your job, or the way you think. It is the beginning of a new 9 year cycle. You should be careful with your finances. You may change your eating habits, improving your health. It is important to have physical activities. You may have constipation, blood pressure problems and mental fatigue. This is the year to clear up hang-ups from your love life in the past. If you act egotistically, you may find the next 9 years difficult. You will be in the 8 house starting February 4 of the year you will be 21 + keep adding 9 years.

9 Fire – brightness – When you are in the 9 house, you will want to be with 9 fires. It is usually a good year, but you need to be aware of extremes that can lead to difficulties. You can get good news, your relationships are active and positive, and you can do what you want to do. For success, you need to act from a firm base. You need to be clear and orderly when carrying new ideas. You need to be calm and to the point. Watch your blood pressure circulation, nervous system, and infectious disease. Be careful around fire. Your love life may flourish, but be careful of superficial people. Do not be too emotional. You will be in the 9 house starting February 4 of the year you will be 22 + keep adding 9 years.

1 Water – darkness or floating – When you are in the 1 house, you will want to be with 1 water's. It is a good time for mental and spiritual development, but not social expansion. You should look to the past and plan for the future. Don't start new projects, and be cautious. You should eat less and avoid extreme yin foods. A previous sickness could come back. You should be careful around water, the extreme cold, and when traveling. In relationships you can easily be misunderstood, causing a good relationship to go bad. Mistakes can cause regrets that last a long time. You will be in the 1 house starting February 4 of the year you will be 23 + keep adding 9 years.

2 Soil – stagnation – When you are in the 2 house, you want to be with 2 soils. Being conservative and listening to others can lead to a good year. Your social expansion slows down; you should not begin a new business. It is a good year for study, improving yourself, and strengthening friendships. You finances may not be good until a latter part of the year. If you eat right and conserve energy, your health can improve. You should be careful in love, watch out for food poisoning, and accidents near water. In the summertime, you are more prone to infections, fevers, or skin diseases. You will be in the 2 house starting February 4 of the year you will be 24 + keep adding 9 years.

3 Tree – proceeding or rising – When you are in the 3 house, you want to be with 3 trees. Your future is active and bright. You need to act quickly to accomplish your goals. It is time to start a new business and is a good year for traveling. To accomplish your goals you should be flexible, optimistic, and modest. Don't eat or drink too much. Eating less in the morning can help you accomplish your

goals. You tend to be lucky in love and may start new relationships. Watch out for accidents, you can experience trouble with your nervous system and liver. You will be in the 3 house starting February 4 of the year you will be 25 + keep adding 9 years.

4 Tree – preparation – When you are in the 4 house, you want to be with 4 trees. You are optimistic and it is a good time for achieving your goals. Previous ventures grow, develop, and prosper. It is better to stay with these ventures and start new ones. Don't be impulsive, stay with what is familiar. You should watch out for bronchitis, digestive, liver, lung, speech, and throat problems. You may become nervous and irritable. Avoid too salty or too much animal foods. Your health this year determines your health for the next 9 years. Previous relationships develop and flourish. It is a good year to establish trust with others. You will be in the 4 house starting February 4 of the year you will be 26 + keep adding 9 years.

81 year cycle: On February 4, 1955, a new 81 year cycle began. This is a 9 Fire cycle. This high energy period collapses many of the institution and ways of thinking established during the previous 1 Water cycle, which started February 4, 1874. It was a period of dictators consolidation of state control WWI and WWII. On February 4, 2036 a 8 Soil cycle begins. It will be a period of change or revolution. The economy, government, medicines, sciences, and society will change and establish into a peaceful world.

120 year cycle: There is a 120 year cycle that marks major epochs of human destiny. The last 120 year period began in 1984. It will end in 2104. This also ends the 25,800 year cycle representing the shifting influence of the constellations over the North Pole. A new age will start with the opposite tendencies of our present. There will be spiritual development and world wide cooperation. The Ki years will go form 1 to 9, instead of 9 to 1. Lifestyles will be reserved and an age of peace will be established lasting 10,000 years. This is the conclusion of over 12,000 years of materialistic yang development starting a new spiritual yin civilization. The earth will change its rotation as the sun does every 10.5 years.

1 Water – The water features are weakened by overprotective parents who repeatedly instill fear, excessive caution and overly strong criticism of them or others which could end up with a fearful and exclusive personality infecting the bladder, kidneys, and possible sex drive. They are often distant with one or both parents, usually the father. Difficult childhood experience tests their patience and drives them toward independence which brings them future success. They have a greater chance at succeeding in their own adventures than in inherited ones. They are independent, talented, and intelligent. They don't like being pushed around or confined to any one thing. They can often relate to a stranger better than their own family. They can develop a wide circle of acquaintances. They may be overconfident and must guard against too great an independence, which could lead to loneliness and isolation. They have difficulty finishing things. They can adapt to any other personality or situation. They are easygoing and agreeable. They are involved in some form of communication and creative work. They may appear general and reserve but they are really strong. They are good listeners, but are good at hiding their true feelings and can keep secrets. They can see both sides of a situation and are great at diplomacy. They are sensitive to other people's feelings. Their actions are deliberate and they make good leaders. They are good at social relations. The wider the range of people, the happier they are. They care for others but may think they are superior. Their interest in the opposite sex may give them many love affairs, but they keep their personal lives confidential. They are good in business.

2, 5, and 8 Soils – The soils are balanced, centered, stabilized, secure, thoughtful, think too much, need to find practical pursuits, outgoing, social, inventiveness, creative thinking, and likes to work with soil. Their balanced-stabilized quality is weakened by a human environment that is unreliable, undependable, irresponsible, or hypocritical, which could cause a child to have an attitude of cynicism and doubt. This could develop spleen, pancreas and stomach problems.

2 Soil – Two soils are interested in music, culture, philosophy, politics, business, and nurturing. They are sincere. They can become too idealistic and impractical. Their success usually comes later in life. They are too sensitive and have a hard time with sudden change. They are detail-minded and are perfectionists, which cause them to prefer doing things themselves than delegate to others. They may make demands of others and may be pushy with their opinions. They don't like to waste time. Their work tends to be around projects with full speed. They are better in professional careers than organizations. Their conversations are around work. They devote themselves to needs of others. They often choose a seven metal mate. They are trustworthy and serious in romance, but the men are sometimes playboys. The women may interfere in other people's business and may become isolated. They may show too much kindness. They are quiet people of action, usually reserved and gentle. They have patience, diligence, and devotion. They need time to develop their careers. They are conservative and build up experience slowly. They can reach their goals by working from the bottom up. They are in a hurry to succeed and want things their own way, which often leads to failure. Patience is a virtue.

5 Soil – Most five soils grow up in difficult family surroundings. They should build their future outside their families and get help from strangers, which installs strength in worldly matters. They want to possess great talent. Some are wild and rough, but are hard workers. Their state of mind is indomitable and has perseverance, especially in business. They have a fatalistic approach to gambling and try to make their fortunes in a single stroke. They are the balanced energy between water and fire. They have clear opinions and character. They are often the center of relationships, business, and of their community. They are the primal power. They pick who they want to be with, nobody can pick them. Others count on them for their viewpoints and guidance. They are clear and respected; they may become self-important, opinionated or egotistical. They are gentle on the outside but strong on the inside. They are realists, practical and hate pointless discussions. They think things out and proceed step by step and it is hard to change their minds. They can find it hard to adapt to new situations. They like knowledge, history, reading and hobbies. They like to think about the past and future. They have confidence and independence, which may make it hard for them to work as a team. They have great willpower and like challenges and new ideas. They are responsible and like to solve their own problems. They have the strength and vitality to create a new life under any circumstances. They are frank and their self-confidence may make them appear detached. They have a way to create their livelihood out of what they like to do. There may be a big age difference in their mate. They are possessive and are usually dedicated to their partner and prefer not to divorce. They shift back and forth between passion and coolness.

8 Soil – Eight soils have a sense of justice. They are serious, silent, deep thinkers, intelligent, optimistic, quiet, and likes to look into things. Their opinions are thought out and firm. Their self reliance may make them isolated or stubborn. They are hard workers. They have good memories and don't make the same mistakes twice. They learn from their mistakes. They are cautious in new relationships, but once they are established, the bonds are deep and long lasting. They may have a middle age crisis but with support from others, they are able to make a rebound. They need good friends for success. They are adventurers and may move often. Many get an inheritance from their

father or grandfather. Because they are gentle on the outside and strong on the inside, they are well-liked. If they become materialistic, people may dislike them. They are good planners and have great ideas. They tend to stick to one partner and it's hard to change their mind. They are steady, not too hot or cold. If they have affairs, they're not usually serious. They are not too passionate or romantic. Independent, it is hard for them to express emotions. Many women remain single. Their self motivation can make them act immature. They want to control relationships, causing jealousy, which they get over quickly. They go back and forth between being greedy and being tender. Changing their minds make people think they are insincere. In romance, they like change and adventure. They take too many chances in money, but are good at figures and saving. With the right help, they will build up their wealth. If they have patience and loyalty to those who help them, their quality of life will improve.

3 and 4 Tree – Trees are emotional, poetic, and idealistic, have long range goals, and have spiritual values. They are artists, have imagination, and are romantics. As a child, they need encouragement, emotional support, appreciation, inspiration, and able to explore curiosities, or they may have tendencies toward anger, with liver and gall bladder damage. They need to have an orderly peaceful life. In extreme cases, they need solitude, surroundings, like the mountains or forest area.

3 Tree – Three trees are brilliant, active, curious, and energetic. To the extreme, they can overlook the most practical parts of life and may have superficial thinking. They may act before they think and have quick tempers. They are often kindhearted. They show their feelings immediately in facial expressions. Their face often becomes flushed. They stick to their opinions and are clear about their likes or dislikes. They express themselves getting to the point and have difficulty lying, which makes them seem opinionated or strong willed. Their minds are quick, and they like to be the best at what they do. They respect their fathers and elders. They are romantic and are attracted to someone pursuing in idealistic dream. From a young age, they are attracted to the opposite sex. They are often too possessive and jealous and need to work on their romantic and emotional feelings. In work, they dislike monotony, but need to devote themselves to one project at a time. They often have failure or success before thirty. In an organization, they are often promoted quickly and have financial success. They have high energy which leads them to many experiences which they pursue eagerly for a time before moving to something else. The creation of new ventures, often finds them success early in life. They make quick decisions without caution, not considering other influences. Because they are on the go, they must develop patience and persistence. Trying to do too much too soon can exhaust their energy. They are open, honest, and insensitive. Because of their frankness, they can alienate others, causing loneliness. Satisfaction is gained by what they did, not through others. They will give their energies to what they want to do and don't want any help. Their relationships can depend on convenience. They are often at odds with their fathers, which makes their approach to life strong. They shouldn't bite off more than they can chew.

4 Tree – Four trees are thoughtful, practical, and have socially oriented goals. They are divided into two groups. The first type is more subdued, is a great analysis and has strong theatrical ability. Many are Nobel Peace Prize winners. The second type is sensitive to other people's feelings and embrace different points of view. They are idealistic but may be impractical and may waste time, energy, and money. Both have a strong desire for freedom and justice, which makes them resist authority. They are eloquent and can agitate or influence others. They can be indecisive and tend to go with the majority regretting it later. They have a hearty laugh and pat people on the back. They are romantic and the men can be playboys. They tend to get married at an early or late age. They may

take financial risks, and experience financial insecurity. They like administrative and management jobs, but not in operating details. They are better at advising and guiding the overall direction of a business. They are attracted to love and romance and often unexpectedly meet their partner. The women attract older men as protectors, and if divorced, usually remarried. Both men and women may miss good opportunities by not making good decisions. They are affectionate, loving, feeling a need to take care of others, and have a large social circle. Their easy, gentle ways, make them appreciated for their communication skills. They often act on their emotions alone. Because they are givers, they have a good reputation and earn the confidence of others. Often their success comes from the results of efforts they made for someone else. They can easily change their minds, which can create problems. Their indecisiveness when something isn't clear creates doubt in confusion, especially in marriage. Their easy appearance may hide their real desires. They are hard to figure out because they seem indecisive on the outside. They should not expect to receive anything from others unless they give first.

6 and 7 Metal – Metals are inwardly directed, self-disciplined, have strength, self-control, likes ethical and orderly behavior, and logical. If confidence is weakened by loneliness and there is no warmth, symphony and compassion, it will end up in depression or melancholy with problems in the lungs and large intestines. Metals need warmth, inspiration, compassion, loving care, sympathy, support, and positive reinforcement. They are disciplined, self-developed, have organizational abilities, and are practical.

6 Metal – Six metals are usually born into their parent's most powerful period. As they grow, the fortunes of their parents tend to decline and they may have it hard until middle age. They have the power to conquer anything by their good attitudes, organizational skills, and minds. They can be too defensive and too cautious, which causes them to lose opportunities. Because they are calculating, they can feel uncomfortable in social situations. Their frankness can offend others unintentionally so they try to be considerate of others. Because of their mind, it is hard for them to compromise quickly. They always do everything their own way, which may cause them to isolate themselves. Their pride makes them think they are always right, but also gives them strength to persevere in hard times. They are clever and intelligent. Because it is hard for them to see other people's views, they may have difficulty in social relations. They are strong willed and act on their beliefs, not others. They dislike defeat, they are not talkative, they make great leaders, they appear to have a lot of pride, but are often insecure. They are skillful in business but may be unhappy if they don't reach the top. They often scold others to impose discipline. People respect them, but often keep their distance. They are honest straight-forward, creative, and may take on too much work. They like machinery, equipment, and challenges. They are conservative thinkers, and are often ruled by their emotions. The women speak and act directly; they are active in romance, but passion rapidly shifts from hot to cold. They are possessive of their mate but may appear disinterested. The men can be intimidated by their wives. The women's professional interest distract from their romantic lives. They need to have a stronger, emotional, or romantic personality.

7 Metal – If seven metals are over-indulged in childhood, they will be spoiled, conceited, and extravagant, which can lead to their demise. They are practical, and well versed, which is often the key to their success. They have common sense and organizational powers. They are very active and they are stylish dressers. They are good at peacemaking and meditating. They can be bossy. They like luxury and dining out. They are often choosy about their partners. They are good workers and good at handling money. They are noticed by seniors, which may help them be promoted to positions of importance.

They have a rich and emotional life. For many, their number one priority is love and romance. They may experience difficulty if they ignore the practical side of relationships. Women often have a naive sex appeal. Their social personalities make them good speakers and entertainers. Their sharp minds are helped by strong, self interested calculations. But they can be nervous. They are flexible and easygoing. They are respected because of their quick wit and sensing what others are thinking. Their optimism can cause them not to finish projects and not to look at their conduct. For their careers, they need to learn independence which will help improve their lives because of their self interest.

9 Fire – Nine fires with repeated overindulgence, being spoiled with no guidance, insincere, undisciplined and overly sentimental parents will cause them to have a tendency to act without thinking, becoming overly developed. This may cause overexcitement, hysterical behavior, and trouble in the heart, triple heater and small intestines. They are active, outgoing, sociable and good at goals that have been established by others. They are good at dealing with the public. They have a clear opinion on just about any topic, even if they don't know what they are talking about. They may tend to act on impulse without thinking. They have knowledge and quick sharp minds. If your opinion is different from theirs, it is hard for them to be your friend. To accomplish their objective, they act positive but may lack kindness. They may be overconfident and are detail minded. They will point out another person's defects, but do not like to be criticized. They are good at public relations. After marriage, they may become self-centered in family relationships. The women often marry men who are more intelligent and socially established. They are more successful pursuing their goals independently. They are often successful financially. They may base their judgments on outer appearances. They have strong preferences and many people like them. They often receive romantic offers but need to watch their step. They need responsibility and discipline. They should regulate their life with a schedule to be more punctual with clear plans for the future. They are kind, generous, openhearted, social and compassionate. They are smart and have foresight and determination. They have leadership skills but should watch out for their indecision, which causes anger. They can act on impulse, not considering others. This may isolate them, especially in times of trouble. To improve their lives, they should be more sincere and not arrogant. They should learn to listen to others. They need consistency, diplomacy, and patience. They can feel that they are superior, which can turn into vanity and lack of consideration of others. With generosity and humbleness, they can accomplish anything.

Reading Faces:
This is not etched in stone. What can change this are your past lives and how your parents raised you.

- Horizontal lines on the forehead – intestines – a broken line means unfinished business
- Vertical lines or dents between the eyes – liver problems – anger
- Blinking more than three times a minute – unstable
- If you can see the whites of the eye on the top or bottom, you are sanpaku which means you are accident prone – Abraham Lincoln, Mahatma Gandhi, JFK, RFK, and MLK were all sanpaku when assassinated.
- Red nose – heart problems
- Mustaches on girls – female problems – black mustaches: too much red meat; white mustache: too much dairy.
- Gap between front teeth – leave home early; the wider the gap, the sooner you leave
- Teeth protruding outward – too much yin food
- Teeth protruding inward – too much yang food

- Crooked teeth – unstable – eating extreme yin and extreme yang foods
- Split in lower lip – leave home early
- Protruding lower lip – colon problems
- Upper lip bigger than lower lip – can be selfish and more apt cheat on their mate
- Cliff chin – likes attention – makes a good actor
- Ears that stick out – stressful or unhappy childhood
- Ears that are flat – stable
- Large earlobes – good constitution
- Darkness around eyes – kidneys – fear – bladder problems – wetting the bed
- Philtrum – dented area below middle of nose and above upper lip – the more pronounced, the higher the fertility rate. The lines inside of the depression is ovary or prostrate problems.

DENTAL CHART

TOP TEETH

Right side teeth:	# 1	# 2 & 3	# 4 & 5	# 6	# 7 & 8
Organs-	Heart Term Ileum Duodenum	Pancreas Stomach Esophagus	Lung Large Intest Bronchi	Liver Gallbladder Billary ducts	Kidney Bladder Ovary/Testicle Prostate/ Uterus Rectum/anus
Joints-	Ulnar side of shoulder, hand and Elbow Plantar side of Foot Toes Sacro-Iliac	Jaw Ant. Hip Ant. Knee Medial Ankle	Radinl side of Shoulder, Hand and Elbow Foot Big Toe	Post. Knee Hip Lat. Ankle	Post. Knee Sacro-coccygeal Post. Ankle
Vertebrae-	C 1, 2, 7 TH 1, 5, 6, 7 S 1, 2	C 1, 2 TH 11, 12 L 1	C 1, 2, 5, 6, 7 TH 2, 3, 4 L 4, 5	C 1, 2 TH 8, 9, 10	C 1, 2 L 2, 3 S 3, 4, 5, SCo
Endocrine-	Ant. Pituitary	Parathyroid (2) Thyroid (3)	Thymus (4) Post pituitary (5)	Intermediate Pituitary Hypothalamus	Pineal
Systems-	Central Nervous and Limbic	Breast	Breast (4)		
Sensory-	Internal Ear Tongue	Oropharynx Larynx Tongue	Nose	Posterior Eye	Nose

	# 1	# 2 & 3	# 4 & 5	# 6	# 7 & 8
Muscles-	Trapezius	Abdominal (2) Latissimus (3)	Diaphragm (4) Pectoralls Maj Clavicular Coracobrachi- alls Popliteus (5)	Deltoid Ant. Serratus	Subcapularis (7) Neck – Flex and Ext (8)
Sinus-		Maxillary	Ethmoid Sinus	Sphenoidal	Frontal Sinus Sphenoidal

Left side teeth:	# 9 & 10	# 11	# 12 & 13	# 14 & 15	# 16
Organs-	Kidney Bladder Ovary/Testicle Prostate/ Uterus Rectum/anus	Livers Biliary ducts	Lung Large Intest. Bronchi	Spleen Stomach Esophagus	Heart Duodenum Jejunum Ileum
Joints-	Post. Knee Sacro- coccygeal Post. Ankle	Post. Knee Hip Lat. Ankle	Radial side of Shoulder, hand and Elbow Foot Big Toe	Jaw Ant Hip Ant Knee Medial Ankle	Ulnar side of Shoulder, hand and Elbow Plantar side of Foot Toes Sacro-Iliac
Vertebrae-	C 1,2 L 2,3 S 3,4,5 SCo	C 1, 2 TH 8, 9, 10	C 1, 2, 5, 6, 7 TH 2, 3, 4 L 4, 5	C 1, 2 TH 11, 12 L 1	C 1, 2, 7 TH 1, 5, 6, 7 S 1, 2
Endocrine-	Pineal	Intermediate Pituitary Hypothalamus	Post Pituitary Thymus (13)	Thyroid (14) Parathyroid (15)	Ant. Pituitary
Systems-			Breast (13)	Breast	Central Nervous and Limbic

	# 9 & 10	# 11	# 12 & 13	# 14 & 15	# 16
Sensory-	Nose	Posterior Eye	Nose	Oropharynx Larynx Tongue	Internal Ear Tongue
Muscles-	Subscapularis (10) Neck – Flex and Ext (9)	Deltoid Ant.Serratus	Diaphragm (13) Pectoralis Maj. Clavicular Coracobra-chialis Popliteus (12)	Abdominal (15) Latissimus (14)	Trapezius
Sinus-	Frontal Sinus Sphenoidal	Frontal Sinus	Sphenoidai	Ethmoid Sinus	Maxillary

BOTTOM TEETH

Right side teeth:	# 32	# 31 & 30	# 29 & 28	# 27	# 26-25
Sinus-		Ethmoidal	Maxillary	Sphenoidal	Frontal Sinus Sphenoidal
Muscles-	Psoas	Quadriceps (31) Gracilis (30) Sartorius (30)	Pect.maj. sternal (29) Quadratus-Lumborum (28) Hamstring	Gluteus maximus	Tensor Fascine-Latae (23) Pyriformis (26) Gluteus medius (25)
Sensory-	Middle Ext. Ear Tongue	Nose	Tongue	Anterior Eye	
Systems-	Peripheral nerves Energy exchange	Arteries (31) Veins (30)	Lymph (29) Breast		
Endocrine-			Ovary and Testicle (28)	Ovary/Testicle	Adrenals

	# 32	# 31 & 30	# 29 & 28	# 27	# 26-25
Vertebrae-	C 1, 2, 7 TH 1, 5, 6, 7 S 1, 2	C 1, 2, 5, 6, 7 TH 2, 3, 4 L 4, 5	C 1, 2 TH 11, 12 L 1	C 1, 2 TH 8, 9, 10	C 1, 2 L 2, 3 S 3, 4, 5 Co
Joints-	Ulnar side of shoulder, elbow and hand Sacro-Iliac Toes Foot plantar side	Radial side of shoulder, elbow and hand Foot Big Toe	Anterior Hip Anterior Knee Medial Ankle Jaw	Posterior Knee Hip Lateral Ankle	Posterior Knee Sacro- coccygeal Posterior Anide
Organs-	Heart Terminal Ileum Ileo-Cecal Area	Large Intestine Ileo-Cecal Area Lung	Esophagus Stomach Pancreas Pylorus Pyloric Antrum	Liver Gall Bladder Biliary Ducts	Kidney Bladder Ovary/Testicle Prosdtate/ Uterus Rectum/Anus

Left side teeth:	# 24 & 23	# 22	# 21 & 20	# 19 & 18	# 17
Sinus-	Frontal Sinus Sphenoidal	Sphenoidal	Maxillary	Ethmoidal	
Muscles-	Tensor Fascine- Latae (23) Pyriformis (23) Gluteus medius (24)	Gluteus maximus	Quadratus- lumborum (21) Pect. maj. sternal (20) Hamstring	Gracilis (19) Sartorius (19) Quadriceps (18)	
Sensory-		Anterior	Tongue	Nose	Middle ext. Ear Tongue
Endocrine-	Adrenals	Ovary/Testicle	Ovary and Testicle (21)		

	# 24 & 23	# 22	# 21 & 20	# 19 & 18	# 17
Vertebrae-	C 1, 2 L 2, 3 S 3, 4, 5 Co	C 1, 2 TH 8, 9, 10	C 1, 2 TH 11, 12 L 1	C 1, 2, 5, 6, 7 TH 2, 3, 4 L 4, 5	C 1, 2, 7 TH 1, 5, 6, 7 S 1, 2
Joints-	Posterior Knee Sacro- coccygeal Posterior Ankle	Posterior Knee Hip Lateral Ankle	Anterior Hip Anterior Knee Medial Ankle Jaw	Radial side of hand, elbow, shoulder Foot Big Toe	Ulnar side of hand, elbow, and shoulder Sacro-Iliac Toes Foot plantar side
Organs-	Kidney Bladder	Liver Biliary Ducts	Esphagus Stomach	Large Intestine Lung	Heart Jejunum
Organs-	Ovary/Testicle Prostate/uterus Rectum/Anus		Spleen	Ileum	

Every tooth is connected to a part of the body though the spinal cord.

ONDAMED®

Ondamed° is a bio-feedback device accordance with Title 21, Chapter 1, Subchapter 1, Part 882, Subpart F, Neurological Therapeutic Device, Section 882.5050. In combination with patients and voluntary control, it offers a highly pacific bio physical analysis application based on electromagnetic inductivity.

This system reinforces treatment currently used including pharmaceuticals, homeopathic remedies, nutritional supplements, and other therapeutic modalities; patients respond faster and with better lasting effect. It will put any practice on the cutting edge of mind to body medicine, ycho-neuro-immunology, and pain management. It has a superior delivery system, a neck applicator placed around the patient's neck, delivers pulse electromagnetic frequencies to the central nervous system. A handheld applicator is used to scan the body and simultaneously deliver therapeutic frequencies to a pacific location, and two matrix applicators address larger areas of the body.

A unique feature is it's reliance upon pulse feedback to monitor patient response to an incoming stimulus. The patient's pulse response indicates which frequency or program would be more therapeutic. Using the pulse feedback, the practitioner rapidly scans the body's preferences, determines the reaction areas in the body, and simultaneously delivers the therapeutic frequencies.

Thermographs taken before and after sessions reveal how quick an inflamed area dissolves; thereby improving the circulation indication by the red/yellow color scheme. It is a comprehensive system integrating electromagnetic frequencies, sound and color to stimulate all senses. During a bio feedback session, the patient may experience a mild tingling sensation, a feeling of release, or nothing at all. A typical session takes about thirty minutes. Patients report leaving a session feeling relaxed and refreshed, being able to think more clearly, and making it better to meet life's challenges. The results include normalization of blood pressure, heart rate, dheacortisol ratios, improve sleep patterns, increase growth hormone release, decrease the muscle tension shift in brainwaves towards alpha and theata states associated with calm mood and creative brain functioning. It also increases production of endorphins, producing a sensation of pleasure, reducing digestive discomforts, associating with stress, reducing of pain and increasing the ability to cope with chronic pain and is anti-inflammatory.

Ondamed° was invented in Schwanau, Germany, by electronics engineer, Rolf Binder, who is well-known for developing Bio-terrain and EAV measurement devices and other medical equipment. It is the end result of twenty-five years of research in biophysical medical testing and therapy. He found out that he could tap into the body's electromagnetic molecular communication, thereby facilitating the natural healing process. The medical professions worldwide have been using it with remarkable success.

The system uses a cutting edge technology that integrates the principles of wave mechanics with the vibrations of biological systems. Wolf Dieter-Kessler, MD has hypothesized that, "each organ and site of the human body has very specific electromagnetic frequencies. If we visualize the body, and its constitute parts as oscillators, in a healthy body, the assembly of the oscillators vibrate in harmony with each other, like a string in a musical instrument. When there is a departure from a healthy synchronous vibration, these parts of the body display a lower energy or a chaotic, asynchronous vibration. Just as micro-magnetic fields expose to induction, impulses produce electron flow, its impulses convert static and blocked, non-regulating areas to dynamic functionality." The most amazing thing about it is that it is AMA approved.

For information on purchasing an **ONDAMED**˙ call Dr. Mark Armstrong, OMD at 770-552-4242.

KING JAMES INSTRUCTIONS
TO CHANGE THE BIBLE

The following is from the 19th century magazine entitled "The Christian Baptist":
From the "Witness," for June 1809.

To the translators of the Bible – with extracts and remarks:

[The following copy of instruction, with the extracts, are taken from Lewis' History of the English Translations of the Bible. They are here inserted, not to introduce the controversy about baptism, but to shew (what is little known) that King James actually forbade the translators of the Bible to translate the words *baptism* and *baptize*, and that these words accordingly are not translated by them. If any of our readers should doubt of the correctness of the extracts made, we refer them to the above work that they may read for themselves.]

"FOR the better ordering of the proceedings of the translators, his Majesty recommended the following rules to them, to be very carefully observed:-

1. The ordinary Bible, read in the church, commonly called the Bishop's Bible, to be followed, and as little altered as the original will permit.

2. The names of the prophets and the holy writers, with the other names in the text, to be retained, as near as may be according as they are vulgarly used.

3. The old ecclesiastical words to be kept; as the word *church*, not to be translated *congregation*, &c.

4. When any word hath divers significations, that to be kept which has been most commonly used by the most eminent fathers, being agreeable to the propriety of the place, and the analogy of faith.

5. The division of the chapters to be altered, either not al all, or as little as may be, if necessity so require.

6. No marginal notes at all to be affixed, but only for the explanation of the Hebrew of Greek words, which cannot, without some circumlocution, so briefly and fitly be expressed in the text.

7. Such quotations of places to be marginally set down, as shall serve for the fit references of one scripture to another.

8. Every particular man of each company to take the same chapter of chapters; and having translated or amended them severally by himself, where he thinks good, all to meet together, to confer what they have done, and agree for their part what shall stand.

9. As any one company hath dispatched any one book in this manner, they shall send it to the rest to be considered of seriously and judiciously: for his Majesty is very careful in this point.

10. If any company, upon the review of the book, so sent, shall doubt or differ upon any places, to send them word thereof to note the places, and therewithal to send their reasons; to which if they consent not, the difference to be compounded at the general meeting, which is to be of the chief persons of each company, at the end of the work.

11. When any place of special obscurity is doubted of, letters to be directed by authority to send to any learned in the land for his judgment in such a place.

12. Letters to be sent from every bishop to the rest of the clergy, admonishing them of this translation in hand, and to move and charge as many as being skillful in the tongues, have taken pains in that kind, to send their particular observations to the company, either at Westminster, Cambridge, or Oxford, according as it was directed before in the king's letter to the archbishop.

13. The directors in each company to be deans of Westminster and Chester, and the king's professors in Hebrew and Greek in the two universities.

14. These translations to be used when they agree better with the text than the Bishop's Bible, viz. Tyndal's, Coverdale's, Matthews', Wilchurch's, Geneva."

"A copy of these orders or instructions being sent to Mr. Lively at Cambridge, and other copies to Dr. Harding, the king's reader of Hebrew at Oxford and Dr. Andrews, dean of Westminster; it seems as if some other doubts arising concerning them, application was made by the vice-chancellor to the bishop of London for the resolution of them. To which his lordship replied that, "to be sure, if he had not signified so much unto them already, it was his Majesty's pleasure that, besides the learned persons employed with them for the Hebrew and Greek, there should be three of four of the most eminent and grave divines of their university assigned by the vice-chancellor, upon conference with the rest of the heads, to be the overseers of the translations, as well Hebrew as Greek, for the better observation of the rules appointed by his Highness, and especially concerning the third and fourth rule; and that when they had agreed upon the persons for this purpose, he prayed them to send him word thereof."

The author from which the above is extracted, observes, that the translators, in their preface to the reader, affixed to their translation, declare as follows: "They had," they said, "on the one side avoided the scrupulosity of the Puritans, who left the old ecclesiastical words and betook them to others, as when they put washing for baptism, and congregation for church: and on the other hand had shunned the obscurity of the Papists, in their Azymes, Tunike, Rational, Holocausts, Prepuce, Pasche, and a number of such like, whereof their late translation (at Doway and Rhemes) was full, and that of purpose to darken the sense; that since they must needs translate the Bible, yet, by the language thereof, it might be kept from being understood." The same author says, "Of this translation the learned Mr. Matthew Poole has given the following character. In this royal version, says he, occur a good many specimens of great learning and skill in the original tongues, and of an acumen and judgment more than common. By others it has been censured as too literal, or following the original Hebrew and Greek too closely and exactly, and leaving too many of the words in the original untranslated, which makes it not so intelligible to a mere English reader. This last was perhaps in some measure owing to the king's instructions, the 3d of which was, that the old ecclesiastical words should be kept. However it be, we see many of the words in the original retained, as Hosannah, Hallelujah, Amen, Raka, Mammon, Manna, Maranatha, Phylactery, &c. for which no reason can be given but that they are left untranslated in the vulgar Latin." This author further declares, that Nary, in his preface to the Bible, (printed in 1719,) remarks, there were certain words in the scripture, which use and custom had in a manner consecrated, as, Sabbath, Rabbi, Baptize, Scandalize, Synagogue, &c. which, he said, he had every where retained, though they were neither Latin nor English, but Hebrew and Greek, because they are as well understood, even by men of the meanest capacity, as if they had been English." Speaking of Wickliffe's translation, he adds, "In Dr. Wickliffe's translation of the Bible, we may observe that those words of the original which have since been termed sacred words, were not always thus superstitiously regarded: thus, for instance, Matt, iii. 6. is rendered weren waschen, instead of were baptized, though, for the most part, they are here left untranslated, or are not rendered into English so frequently as they are in the Angle-Saxonic translation.

From the above instructions given by king James to the translators, and the subjoined extracts, the following observations are obvious, and are submitted to the consideration of the disciples of Jesus Christ.

1. It is evident from rule third of the king's instructions to the translators, that he forbade them to translate the old ecclesiastical words; and in rule fourth he commands, that when any word hath divers significations, they should retain that in their translation which has been most commonly used by the most eminent fathers, being agreeable to the propriety of the place and the analogy of faith.

From the first extract subjoined to the above instructions of the king, it appears that hid Majesty was careful that his instructions should be observed by the translators, and especially the third and fourth rules. "It was his Majesty's pleasure, that besides the learned persons employed with them for the Hebrew and Greek, there should be three or four of the most eminent engraved divines of their university assigned by the vice-chancellor, upon conference with the rest of the heads, to be overseers of the translations, as well Hebrew as Greek, for the better observation of the rules appointed by his Highness, and especially concerning the third and fourth rules." In the second extract, the translators, in their preference to the reader, declare that they had observed at least his Majesty's third rule respecting the old ecclesiastical words. They say, they had "on the one side avoided the scrupulosity of the Puritans, who left the old ecclesiastical words and betook them to others, as when they put washing for baptism," &c. In the third extract, though highly commended (and we believe justly) by Mr. Poole, their translation was censured by some others. The grounds of this censure are, that their translation is "too literal, or following the original Hebrew and Greek too closely and exactly, and leaving too many of the words in the original untranslated, which makes it not so intelligible to a mere English reader." It is said by the author from whom the instructions and extracts were taken, that "this was perhaps in some measure owing to the king's instructions, the third of which was, that the old ecclesiastical words should be kept." He adds, that "however it be, we see many of the words in the original retained, as, hosanna, &c. for which no reason can be given but that they are left untranslated in the vulgar Latin." This author also informs us that Nary, in his preface to the Bible, printed 1719, says, that "he had every where retained these consecrated words, though they were neither Latin nor English, but Hebrew and Greek." And he adds in the last extract, that Dr. Wickliffe, in his translation, though he has in Matt. iii. 6. rendered the word *baptized* by *washed*, yet these words termed sacred words, are, for the most part, left untranslated by him, or are not so frequently translated into English as in the Angle-Saxonic translation.

2. Let it be particularly noticed, that among those words called consecrated ecclesiastical words, and which were forbidden by the king to be translated into English, are the words baptism and baptize. This must be obvious to any person who will compare the king's instructions with the extracts made above. The king, in his instructions to the translators, rule third, commands "the old ecclesiastical words to be kept," and gives the word church not to be translated congregation, with an &c. as a specimen of these words. The translators, in their preface quoted above, declare that they, in order to avoid being puritanical in their translation, had put baptism where the Puritans had put washing. They also say that the Puritans, by so doing, "left the old ecclesiastical words," which clearly demonstrate that the word baptism was one of those words reckoned both by the king and the translators, to be an old, a consecrated, and an ecclesiastical word. This, the translators add, was one of the Puritan scrupulosities, and that they had, in their translation, avoided it. This is also proved from what was said by Nary in his preface to the Bible, printed 1719. He declares, in the extract made above, that baptize was one of the consecrated words which he had every where retained in his translation, and which he allows are neither Latin nor English, but Greek. If more evidence of this fact was necessary, we might add that the author of the work from which the extracts above are made, declares that these words called sacred words (of which baptism and baptize are two) were not always thus superstitiously regarded. As evidence of this, he remarks that Dr. Wickliffe, in his translation of Matthew iii.6. rendered the phrase were baptized by weren waschen, though, in his translation, the

old ecclesiastical words are, for the most part, left untranslated, or are not rendered into English so frequently as they are in the Anglo Saxonic translation.

3. From the above instructions and extracts, it is very evident that whatever the words baptism and baptize may signify in the Greek language, they are words which are not translated in our version of the Bible. The king virtually prohibited their being translated, the translators declare they left them untranslated, and others allow that they are neither "Latin nor English," but Greek. This surely should rouse the attention of every one who has any regard to the authority of the Divine Saviour, to inquire what do these words mean when correctly translated into English. If they signify sprinkling or pouring let them be so translated. Had the king and the translators been Baptists, and believed that these words signified immersion or dipping, would it not have been singular that they should agree to conceal their meaning by giving us only the Greek words anglicized? If they did mean sprinkling, as is generally asserted, there surely could have been no harm in translating them accordingly, when it was both the duty and interest of those who superintended the translation to do it. Why, then, all this concealment of their signification? It is said that they were old, ecclesiastical, and even consecrated words. It is believed that, consecrated and ecclesiastical as the king and translators esteemed them, had they meant any thing but immersion, these qualities would not have saved them from being rendered into English. But who said these words were consecrated and ecclesiastical words, which should not be translated? The king and ecclesiastics, whose practice required this pious fraud to justify their kind of baptism, or at least to conceal that their practice was unscriptural. In no place of the Bible, that I remember, does God say that there are certain old, consecrated, and ecclesiastical words, which must not be translated into the English language. The translators themselves only thought that these words were consecrated and ecclesiastical, when they occurred in certain places, and when used to express the mode of christian baptism. Thus, in the following passages, where the same Greek words occur, they disregard their age, their consecration, and the ecclesiastical nature. "He it is to whom I shall give a sop when I have dipped it. And when he had dipped the sop, he gave it to Judas Iscariot, the son of Simon." "And he was clothed with a vesture dipped in blood, and his name was called the Word of God." John xiii. 26. Rev. xix. 13. See also Matt. xxvi. 23. in the Greek. The translators in these, and in other instances, have inadvertently, or rather unavoidably, to make sense of these passages, shewn us that they believed the Greek word baptisma means dipping. It may be presumed that there were particular reasons for leaving these words untranslated where christian baptism is spoken of, unless we can make ourselves believe that in those days king James and the translators in this acted without any reasons at all. But it is not easily believed that they acted without these reasons, when it is remembered that they had every inducement to translate the words if they meant nothing contrary to their practice. It was with these old ecclesiastical words that the clergy succeeded in preserving the fascination of priestcraft. When Tyndal issued his translation of the Bible, because he had in it disregarded the words which the clergy esteemed sacred, they condemned it. He has, for instance, changed charity into love; church into congregation; priest into senior; grace into favor; confession into knowledge; penance into repentance; and a contrite heart into a troubled heart. Sir Thomas Moore, who warmly espoused the cause of the clergy against Tyndal's translation, wrote a dialogue, with a view to bring it into contempt among the people. Tyndal, in answer to it, (as quoted by the author from whom we have taken our extracts) thus speaks: "What made them whose cause Sir Thomas espoused, so uneasy and impatient, was, they had lost their juggling terms wherewith they imposed on and misled the people. For instance, the word church, he said, was, by the popish clergy, appropriated to themselves; whereas, of right, it was common to all the whole congregation of them that believe in Christ. So, he said, the school-doctors and preachers were wont to make many divisions, distinctions, and sorts of grace; with confession, they juggled and made the people, as oft as they spake of it, to understand it by shrift in the ear. So by the word penance, they made the people

understand holy deeds of their enjoining, with which they must make satisfaction for their sins to Godward." The Bible is not yet free from these juggling terms, when words are left untranslated and another meaning is affixed to them than what they originally signify, and that meaning sanctioned by very extensive practice. Whether this has originated in kingcraft or priestcraft, or in both, justice demands that it should be detected. A sacred regard to the authority of God ought to lead us to reject an error, however old, sanctioned by whatever authority, or however generally practised.

Before the King James Version (1611), there was Wiclif (1380), Tyndal (1534), Cranmer (1539), Geneva (1557), and Rhelms (1582).

In 1557 John Calvin, joined by a small band of Englishmen who had fled the persecutions of "Bloody Mary", undertook to translate the entire Bible into English. This Bible, which became known as the Geneva Bible, was printed constantly from 1560 to 1644 in over 200 different printings, without the supervision or intervention of government. Other Bibles in the Geneva Project transformed the Netherlands, France, Northern Italy, and Iceland.

With the 199 edition of the Geneva Bible, the thousands of margin notes reached saturation. Later editions added no more of these study guides. These margin notes, also called "glosses", were quoted well after 1611 by King James' churchmen, who found them to be an indispensable tool for studying the Sacred Texts.

The Geneva Bible was the Bible of choice for William Shakespeare and John Milton. The 1599 edition was the Bible the Pilgrims held at Plymouth Rock in 1620 and is thought to be the Bible consulted at our Constitutional Convention in 1787.

The margin notes of John Calvin, John Knox, Miles Coverdale, William Wittingham at al so infuriated King James that the Geneva Bible was, for a time, banned in England. King James called it "seditious" and made its ownership a felony. The Bishop's Bible was introduced in competition but it failed to win popular support. Eventually, in 1611, James introduced the "Authorized" King James Version. The King James Version relies heavily on the Geneva Bible, however, minus the margin notes that enraged the King and his servants in the church.

The 1599 Geneva Bible was the foundation upon which our Christian American Republic. Jesus was a Hebrew, not a Jew and Nazareth did not exist in Jesus' time.

SPIRITUAL POWER

The Alkaline-forming state of being:

The alkaline-forming state of being is driven neither by anxiety nor ambition. Recognition and fame may come however, because the inherent nature of love has been realized. From this realization, proper alkalinity continuously permeates the physical body.

The secret of establishing and maintaining an alkaline-forming state of being is devotion in the form of service to others. This does not mean that you must give everything you have away or run around being a "do-gooder." The act of service is often misjudged. It is not always a world shaking humanitarian project. It is generally the essential way you treat your neighbor and yourself.

A warm loving smile for someone who feels all is lost and is forlorn, the sincere touch to the hand of someone who is desperate, a monetary offering to someone in need, the kind word or prayer for an animal in pain, the heartfelt blessings for the food you prepare, joyously helping a neighbor mend a fence, a good belly laugh with a physically sick friend, are only a few examples of service to others.

Serve with this thought in mind – to manifest the highest and best in yourself in every way. A truly alkaline-forming state of Being is internally rich, peaceful and content. Alkalinity then will flow in the body, sweeten life and lift you in to the heavens.

The Healer's Prayer:

> Our Father, who are within
> Hallowed be thy name.
> Thy kingdom come; Thy will be done
> On earth, as it is within.
> Give us this day, our selfless intent.
> Forgive us of our self centeredness
> As we project love to others.
> And lead us not into temptation,
> But deliver us from envy.
> For thine is the kingdom within
> And the glory without

Place a written copy of the 91st Psalm over your door on the inside of your house. This will protect people leaving and entering your home. Place mistletoe in a small bag above the door in your home next to your 91st Psalm, or at various places around your home, for added protection. Place a small mirror at the entrance of your house so visitors will look into it when entering. This will prevent evil spirits from entering your house.

Psalm 91

¹ He who dwells in the shelter of the Most High
 will rest in the shadow of the Almighty.

² I will say of the LORD, "He is my refuge and my fortress,
 my God, in whom I trust."

³ Surely he will save you from the fowler's snare
 and from the deadly pestilence.

⁴ He will cover you with his feathers,
 and under his wings you will find refuge;
 his faithfulness will be your shield and rampart.

⁵ You will not fear the terror of night,
 nor the arrow that flies by day,

⁶ nor the pestilence that stalks in the darkness,
 nor the plague that destroys at midday.

⁷ A thousand may fall at your side,
 ten thousand at your right hand,
 but it will not come near you.

⁸ You will only observe with your eyes
 and see the punishment of the wicked.

⁹ If you make the Most High your dwelling—
 even the LORD, who is my refuge-

¹⁰ then no harm will befall you,
 no disaster will come near your tent.

¹¹ For he will command his angels concerning you
 to guard you in all your ways;

¹² they will lift you up in their hands,
 so that you will not strike your foot against a stone.

¹³ You will tread upon the lion and the cobra;
 you will trample the great lion and the serpent.

¹⁴ "Because he loves me," says the LORD, "I will rescue him;
 I will protect him, for he acknowledges my name.

[15] He will call upon me, and I will answer him;
    I will be with him in trouble,
    I will deliver him and honor him.

[16] With long life will I satisfy him
    and show him my salvation.

For protection against AIDS, Dioxin, Epstein-Barr, and many other diseases, males should take fifteen mustard seeds a day, and ten for females.

For a more peaceful sleep, put a feather from a peaceful bird under your pillow.

Other powerful scriptures:

- Isaiah 53:5 – For healing, say three times in a row, three times daily: "By his stripes thou shall be healed."
- Ezekiel 16:6 – Repeat three times to stop bleeding.
- Psalm 142:5 – This Psalm protects us from a dangerous viroid that is rapidly being spread around. A viroid is an infectious particle 150 times smaller than a virus. They can cause extreme illness. Write this Psalm out and carry it with you, the vibration of the written word protects you.
- Psalm 58 – Use this to break up dark forces.
- Psalm 48 – this is the antidote for Epstein-Barr.

PLAY IT AGAIN SAM

Einstein discovered energy is equal to the mass times the speed of light times the speed of light ($E=MC^2$). This means that energy cannot be destroyed, but changes form. Your soul is immortal energy. If it can come into a body once, it can do it again. Even though many religions do not teach it, it is one of your many talents.

For God to be a just God there has to be reincarnation. The Bible teaches vengeance is God's and he will repay. All karma must be balanced out with dharma. For Adolph Hitler it will probably take 100 lifetimes. For Joseph Stalin it will probably take 200 lifetimes.

Jesus said, "I am not of this world." There is no one on this planet that is of this world. We are all spiritual beings inhabiting planet Earth to learn. The key is to learn without bringing karma into your next lifetime. That's why Jesus said, "Forgive them for they know not what they do".

Luke 12:1 – In the mean time, when there were gathered together an innumerable multitude of people, insomuch that they trode one upon another, he began to say unto his disciples first of all, Beware ye of the leaven of the Pharisees, which is hypocrisy.

Luke 12:2 – For there is nothing covered that shall not be revealed; neither hid, that shall not be known.

Luke 12:3 – Therefore, whatsoever ye have spoken in darkness shall be heard in the light; and that which ye have spoken in the ear in closets shall be proclaimed upon the housetops.

The spirit world knows everything. Nobody gets away with anything. Whatever happens to you depends on your contract which everyone has with God. You are born in the country and have the race, sex and body you need to fulfill the lessons in your contract. Just because you are one race or sex in one lifetime doesn't mean you will be that race in the next. Do unto others as you would have them do unto you, because you are doing it to yourself.

Example: If you murder a six year old child, God will ask for a volunteer to be your child. You will love that child more than anything. It will die, causing you the same pain and suffering that you caused teaching you not to murder.

Who you persecute is who you will probably be with in the next lifetime. This is why I only hate Victoria Secret models and rich people. My sister hates movie stars and Chip n Dales dancers.

Only one in twenty five people in the world get to own their own body. Some people think that the Jews are the chosen people. The only Jews that are chosen are the ones born in America. The Beatles wrote and in the end the love your take is equal to the love you make. The same goes with pain and persecution. If you take away someone's God given Rights, and there is no injured party, you probably won't own your own body in the next lifetime. Without freedom, your soul cannot learn very much except that freedom is everything. You will turn into Patrick Henry Jr. and the theme of your next lifetime will be "Give Me Liberty, Or Give Me Death". The lesson you will learn is not to take away anybody's God given Rights.

The way Americans got to be the chosen people was by God making George Washington bulletproof to establish the Constitution. George Washington could have been King, but instead gave everyone in America all the rights of a King, and that's a lot of rights. You have special rights as an American – Shaffer v. Heitner, 433 U.S. 186, 97 S. Ct. 2569, 53 L. Ed. 2d 683 (1977). However, with the 14th Amendment you are giving up God given Rights for privileges and supporting the ten planks of communism.

Because of the "missing lucky" 13th Amendment of the Constitution, every law since the 1830s is an illegal law, including the second 13th Amendment, every Amendment after it, and every Supreme Court Justice picked by the illegal lawyer Congress. The reason is because it was made by "titles of nobility" (Lawyers), who are not American citizens. Lawyers, as members of the British Accreditation Registry (BAR Association) are under British rule. Lawyers in Congress who take the oath to uphold the Constitution are in violation of the oath as soon as they take it.

In other words this Amendment voids all laws made by lawyers giving us a way to go back to a Republic the way God intended it to be. To be against this is to be against God. Will you be one of the chosen people in your next lifetime or will you be in a third world country? Vengeance is God's and he will repay through karma.

"Doing well by doing good." Benjamin Franklin